THESE STORIES SAVED MY LIFE

Furahaa Saba

innovativeink
PUBLISHING
A Division of Kendall Hunt

Cover image © Shutterstock.com

www.innovativeinkpublishing.com
Send all inquiries to:
4050 Westmark Drive
Dubuque, IA 52004-1840

Dedication

This collection of stories is dedicated to honor the memory of my mother Mrs. Bernice Roberts Pringle and my grandmother Mrs. Dilsie Brown Roberts.

Remembering Africa, the ancestral home of Black people.

Mary Hudson, a descendant of the Choctaw Nation, is the Native American matriarchal guardian of this collection of stories.

Mary Hudson, the Choctaw Native American Matriarch of the Ramah family.

Table of Contents

Thank You ix

Introduction xi

Chapter 1: Country Love 1

Chapter 2: Stolen Moments Lost Innocence 13

Chapter 3: Lacy Bottom Reader 21

Chapter 4: Passage into White Hands 27

Chapter 5: The Coming Out of Mr. Little's Spirit 33

Chapter 6: The Flower Lady 39

Chapter 7: Rock-Solid Resolve 45

Chapter 8: Chinaberry Playmates 55

Chapter 9: Bright Blue House 63

Chapter 10: Fundamental Terror 69

Chapter 11: Crawling to Safety 79

Chapter 12: Whispers behind the Pine Trees 85

Thank You

Thank you for everything you did to help me bring this book to life:

Venius Adams
Denise Bradshaw
Brian Davis
Trice Effling
Derek Emery
Terri Fowler
Rachel Hilliard
Queenie Hudnall-Hall
Bessie Hudnall
Madeline Hudnall
Angela Hunter
Roz King
Deepa Maria Mazzi
Millie McCoo
Patty Mittendorff
Stephanie Mood
D.A. Servicing
Mikel Taxer
Roxanne Tuscany

Introduction

I started writing *These Stories Saved My Life* in 1989. At the time I was on the faculty in the Communications Department at Salisbury State University. I lived in a small town, Hebron, Maryland, on the outskirts of Salisbury. I wanted to remember my Mississippi roots. So much of the rural community I lived in reminded me of the country life of my hometown Meridian, Mississippi.

This work is a work of creative fiction. It is a mixture of truth and imagination. I learned to allow the main characters to speak through me. It was quite a journey of discovering what people and experiences were hidden in my mind. I am grateful to the people and situations that inspired the writing. Combining imagination and memory brought onto paper the life lessons that formed the basis of my philosophy and outlook on life.

Over the years I have shared, through oral interpretation, this work with different audiences. By sharing the stories, I have learned the value of inspiring conversations about race with different audiences.

Some of the characters and situations are sensitive. It was my intention to heal myself of the pain that I had forgotten was buried in my heart. I hope, through reading, you will gain insight into the unique way life teaches each one of us.

My mom taught me to "Always remember where you came from." This work reflects her teaching.

It is my hope that you will find the reading worthy of your mind and heart. Perhaps a healing moment will rise for you also.

Furahaa Saba
San Diego, California
June 2024

1

Country Love

Prologue

When cotton was king: Black people picking cotton.

Upstate Forever: A Nonprofit Land Conservation Organization
Excerpts from an article by Megan Burton
February 20, 2021

Just after the turn of the 20th century, Black agriculture was at its peak in America. While the eras of Emancipation and Reconstruction were still recent history, African Americans—largely formerly enslaved people and their descendants—had acquired as much as 14 million acres of land across the United States.

Just a century later, however, that number had dwindled. 90 percent of the land amassed by Black farmers across the country had been lost[1]. And this is according to the most recent U.S. Department of Agriculture (USDA) Census, which was completed in 2017.

The reasons for this steep decline in Black land ownership vary. Of course, the overall decrease in small scale agriculture over the past 150 years is a contributing cause, as is the Great Migration, during which millions of African Americans left the rural South for opportunities in the North, Midwest, and American West.

Black Farmers Faced Discrimination

But more sinister factors were also at play. Discriminatory federal policies and financial lending practices are well documented. Black farmers were often denied access to USDA programs managed by locally elected boards.[5]

In addition to systemic institutional discrimination, African American landowners faced the lasting pervasive racism of many of their neighbors in the South. In some cases, this resulted in the forceful, violent taking of their land.

Country Love

Hathor Brown was born to economically deprived Black sharecropping parents on April 1, 1892, in Kemper County, Mississippi. The history books say that Kemper County was created by an act of the Mississippi Legislature on December 31, 1833. The area was formed out of that portion of the Choctaw Cession under the Dancing Rabbit Creek Treaty.

The original family of Mama Hathor.

The first inhabitants of Kemper County were the Choctaw, Chickasaw, Alabama, and Muscogee Indians. The county is located on the central eastern border of Mississippi. Land in the area was developed in the 19th century by White planters to cultivate cotton. Enslaved African Americans were the labor force.

Kemper County is situated in a rich timber section of Mississippi. In 1833, Reuben Kemper, a soldier in the War of 1812, took possession of about 752 square miles of rich farmland. Records show the land was registered as Kemper County on December 23, 1833.

"Bloody Kemper County," as it is often called, is the epitome of rural Mississippi. The label, "Bloody Kemper County," is rooted in the historic battles between the Native Americans and the European immigrants. In addition to instigating battles with the Native American for the purpose of seizing their lands, White immigrants bought and enslaved people of African descent to transform the untamed fertile earth into man-made farmland.

The objective for all of these maneuvers was to feed the desire for wealth. Kemper County was and is a confederate stronghold. One of its historical landmarks is the home of former U.S. Senator John C. Stennis.

Mrs. Ann Woodson, Chancery Clerk in mid-1990 reported, "The courthouse was burned twice before 1915. All the records were destroyed. In those days, if someone was coming to court, and they thought they were going to lose, they just set a fire, and burned the whole place down."

The descendants of enslaved people who still live in Kemper County can talk your ear off about the lynchings, murders, or disappearances of family members. People still talk about horrors of jailed Black prisoners. It is said that screams of torture could be heard from the streets of DeKalb, the county seat.

Although Miss Hathor Brown was a descendant of enslaved people, her father was a landowner. In fact, he donated about 200 acres to the community to build Black Water Baptist Church and adjoining school.

Eventually, the White folks took over most of the land. They did leave enough land for a Black church and cemetery, which still exist today.

The small-framed coco-brown woman already had two children when Mr. Lebni Ramah asked for her hand in marriage. Lebni could not read or write. He did not know his birthdate. But he was a hard-working single man with no children that anyone knew about. His family had abandoned him when he was about 11 years old. His father had an argument with a landowner. It was an act that could get the whole family killed by lynching or other violent methods.

The senior Mr. Ramah took his wife and six of the oldest children and fled in the night. They left the remaining five boys and one girl to raise themselves. The older children had been taken because they could work the fields to support the family. Lebni was the oldest of the children left in the backwoods of central Mississippi. He grew up raising and supporting his younger brothers and sister.

Toward the end of January in 1929 as the depression reached the people of "Bloody Kemper County," Hathor heard people talking about a morally loose woman Lula Bell. Folks were saying that Lula

Bell had left her six-week-old baby in her house by itself while she went to party at a local whiskey house.

Hathor heard this gossip at Black Water Baptist Church on a Sunday morning. After church, she went to the house to see if the people were telling the truth. When you entered the big old house, she heard a child crying. The baby girl, who was later named Ginger, was sucking on the air of the empty bottle Lula Bell had left for her.

Mama Hathor told this story to Topaz many times. She wanted the young girl to know her natural born grandmother. Topaz felt heartbroken for her mother's beginning in life. At the same time, this increased her love and appreciation for her mother and grandmother Hathor. She never felt any abandoned feelings from them. They showed her the true meaning of love throughout her life.

With a deep sense of humility and pride, Mama Hathor told Topaz, "It was cold and dark in that house. I picked Ginger up and wrapped her in my coat. I brought her back to my house. It was bitterly cold that day. I didn't care. I held your mama close to my breast. She was my new baby."

Mrs. Hathor Brown Ramah took the child inside where she fed and bathed her. Finally, Ginger, which she decided to name her, stopped crying, and went to sleep. The older children May and Shaut finished their day. Mrs. Ramah waited for her husband to come home.

It was Sunday, and as usual, there was no telling where Lebni Ramah was. Lebni was a stocky, muscular, easygoing, brown-colored Black man. He was full of love but stern in manner. He did not go to church. He despised preachers for reasons he never explained. Unlike many other homes, when the preacher came for supper at the Ramah home, Lebni insisted that the children eat first. "A preacher ain't worth two bits," was all he said.

Lebni was a man who did not believe in so-called organizations. He held the American value of individual achievement close to his heart. After all, his own parents had abandoned him. It was a scar that cut deep into his soul. He rarely talked about it, but he had a reservoir of deep pain. But he knew how to make and keep an eternal commitment. He spoke his mind and did not take crap from anyone. He could easily have lost his life in the rural backwoods of Mississippi, with either Black or White men or women, because he was direct in his speech. He explained that he had stopped going to church because "There are too many women wearing different kinds of perfumes." The conflicting aromas assaulted his sense of smell. Rather than tolerate the attack, he stopped going to church.

The Sunday Ginger came home with Hathor, Lebni came in and took off his wool suit, which he wore year-round, and the necktie that Hathor teased him about; "You think you somethin' cause you got that strang 'round yo' neck," she smiled at him. On this particular January Sunday, he looked at the baby girl lying in his bed and didn't say a word.

He sat down to his supper of collared greens, corn bread, fried chicken, and his favorite, baked sweet potatoes. He drank the fresh buttermilk he loved, and watched his wife, waiting for her to explain the elephant in their bedroom.

Hathor took her time. She knew his pride and hardworking ways and their circumstances. It was the Great American depression. Everything they had to eat came from their own hands. There was not even spare money for corn meal, flour, sugar, and other basic household goods. She sat in the rocking chair across from her husband. She crossed her slender brown legs right over left and folded her praying hands in the same direction. "Lebni, when I was at church this morning, I heard the folks talking about Lula Bell and how she had left this baby…." He listened, even though he had heard the story down at the store where he had been smoking cigars and having a sip of moonshine whiskey. When Hathor finished her story, Lebni Ramah said simply, "Uhum."

Lebni went to bed knowing his wife had done the right thing. The child wouldn't be abandoned as he had. Hathor and Lebni loved and raised Ginger, and eventually her two daughters, as family.

Hathor and Lebni Ramah were deeply respectful people. They understood each other's role in their relationship. Lebni made the money. Hathor ran the house. It was just that simple.

On Monday morning after Lebni left, and the Ramah children were gone, Hathor wrapped the baby up and went back down to Lula Bell's house.

Hathor knocked on Lula Bell's door. No answer. She knocked again. No answer. Finally, she opened the unlocked door and saw Lula Bell lying on a sheet-less cot by the fire.

Hathor went over and gently shook the young mother. Lula Bell had three older boys that her parents were raising. Her old mixed Choctaw and Black mother had warned Lula Bell, "If you have any more children you will have to raise them yourself."

Hathor could smell the stench of leftover liquor on Lula Bell's body. "I got yo' baby," Hathor said tilting the child toward its natural mother. "Lebni and me gonna keep it. But you have to come and see her. She gonna know who you is. I'm gonna make sure she knows you, cause you her mama."

Hathor turned around and walked out as easily as she had come in. She braved the weather one more time and took the child home to safety.

Hathor told Topaz this story many times. It was her way of re-membering what had happened. Also, it was her way of letting Topaz know how much she loved Ginger.

Topaz knew that Mama Hathor loved her also. She knew this from the tender care her grandmother extended to her in the food she cooked, her mild-mannered and patient way. Topaz knew that by telling her about her history, it was giving the child knowledge of herself.

This knowledge was invaluable. It gave Topaz a foundation to stand on. Her family had come a long way from Africa, through slav-ery, through sharecropping, to eventually become landowners.

Although Ginger was safe, from the beginning of her life, she was damaged. Ginger lived with Hathor and Lebni until they passed away. Ginger loved them as dearly as they loved her. She stayed with them and raised two of her own children in their home.

Hathor and Lebni never officially adopted Ginger. Back in those days, people just took children in when they could. Occasionally,

Lula Bell would come to visit her daughter. It was only after the children were teasing Ginger at school that Hathor told her that Lula Bell was her natural mother. The children at school taunted Ginger, "You ain't got no mama."

Ginger came home traumatized, from school because the children were teasing her. Hathor decided to tell her the whole story of her encounter with Lula Bell. If too much time had passed between visits, Hathor would take Ginger to see her mother, "You need to know who yo' folk is," she told the growing child.

Ginger's visits to her mother were painful. Once she saw a doll lying on the fluffy pillows at Lula Bell's house. Even though Lula Bell was known as a party woman, she also had a reputation as an excellent housekeeper. Her home was meticulous. One day when Ginger was visiting, she saw a doll that she liked. She asked her natural born mother if she could have the doll, "Naw, gal, I ain't givin' you, my thangs," Lula Bell screamed.

Ginger never forgot the gesture of rejection. She told Topaz the story, so that her daughter would know how her natural mother had treated her. She reinforced Mama Hathor's teaching, that a child needs to know the truth of their background, Ginger was a tremendous help to Hathor and Lebni. She had a quick mind, and a strong body. Coupled with her intense personality, she was a perfect addition to the Ramah family.

The Ramahs had very little money and lots of love. Children laughed at the homemade biscuits, with fresh meat in a tin bucket that Hathor sent to school for Ginger's lunch. The meat usually came from the smokehouse that Papa Lebni had built. He trapped wild game when he could find it, like squirrel, beaver, or opossum, to make sure there was some kind of meat in the house. Hathor raised chickens to supplement what Lebni caught in the wild.

In later years, Ginger would recount to her daughter Topaz the shame and pride she felt during the last thanksgiving she spent in school. "All the children were talking about what they were going to have for Thanksgiving dinner. Some were having ham, turkey, roast," she told Topaz. I knew we would have plenty of vegetables like peas and greens, because we grew them in our garden. But we didn't have any money to buy any kind of meat. I was so sad when I went home Wednesday before Thanksgiving."

When Ginger got home, Hathor was baking sweet potato pies, and a pound cake. In a big dishpan, the aging woman was soaking collard greens. When Lebni came home, he sat and watched his wife. He felt the pain of not having money to buy a turkey, or ham, or any kind of meat.

He went and got his shotgun. He sat on the back porch watching for some kind of animal to shoot for meat. Hathor and Ginger saw the squirrel run up the big pear tree in the back yard. Ginger told Topaz this story one time. "Papa stood the gun up against the porch and went over and leaned up against the pear tree. The squirrel ran up the tree further, but Papa caught him by the tail. He pulled the squealing squirrel toward him. The small wild animal was a fighter. The squirrel curved his body toward Papa Lebni and started biting his hands. That squirrel ate Pap's hand's up, but Papa held the squirrel until he could break his neck."

Ginger continued, "Papa skinned the squirrel and brought him into the house. Mama Hathor dressed Papa's bit up hand. Then she started preparing the squirrel for baking. I was so happy; I would have something to tell the children at school about our Thanksgiving dinner. Everything was so good," Ginger told Topaz. Ginger was in the sixth grade at this time. Soon after, she quit school.

Topaz felt this was her mother's way of reminding her not to take food for granted. Ginger worked hard to make sure there was always plenty of food in the Ramah home. She was also letting the young girl know that education was of utmost importance. Ginger's hard work was also directed toward making sure Topaz was educated. She told her daughter, when she was a teenager, "I made up my mind; I was going to buy you the best education I could afford. Get your education so you won't have to work so hard. Remember school and boys do not mix."

Topaz appreciated her mother's sacrifice for her. She completed her master's degree and spent her adult life teaching other people, because she knew education had saved her from the fields and menial labor of Mississippi.

Topaz was grateful her mother shared this story with her. She would always remember it and be grateful for the bounty of food her mother kept for the family.

It wasn't just that Ginger had plenty of food in the house. It was also a blessing that she learned how to prepare a wide variety of foods. She learned from the restaurant she worked in, and from the people she met. She had a gift for preparing food, and she shared her gift openly.

Topaz was proud of this fact. Whenever she went to her mother's home, she knew that would be a loving share of food from Ginger's labor. There was no shortage of what Topaz liked to eat.

Hathor's two older children married and left home early. Her oldest Shaut hired himself out to various jobs until he met and married Sally. They had three children. Like his father, Shaut wanted a piece of land of his own. He worked long enough to buy a small plot. The White people who lived around him did not like the fact that Shaut bought the land.

Mama Hathor told Topaz, "We don't know who did it, but somebody set the house on fire. Shaut his wife and three children were burned to death." This was Hathor's way of letting Topaz know the truth of the suffering she had endeared.

"The Black undertaker would not bury them. He said they had not paid their insurance. I knew that was not true. I went with Sally when she paid the bill. I paid my bill, and she paid her bill on the same day. You could see in the book, where he had tore the page out," Mama Hathor told Topaz.

"The folks said it was some white folks that burned them up. We scrapped enough money together to get one casket. We buried all five of them in the same casket," she shared with a sad voice.

"There is some mean White folks," she told Topaz. There is some mean Black folks too," she told the girl.

Topaz figured Mama Hathor was teaching her about her history, and also teaching her to judge people by their behavior and not their skin color. This teaching and her behavior helped Topaz learn to mingle in diverse people situations.

Mama Hathor's older daughter, May, got married and had 12 children. She lived close by Mama Hathor. May and her children stayed in touch with Mama Hathor. Sometime Mama Hathor would visit with them.

The challenges of life took their toll on Ginger. In her mid-30s, she became an alcoholic. She was a hard worker and was devoted to her adopted parents. Then sometime the pressure would lead her to drink. She drank scotch whiskey. Eventually, she went to Alcoholic Anonymous and became sober.

Topaz was deeply relieved when her mother stopped drinking. Ginger's drinking days were hard and dark for the Ramah family. However, through the grace of love, they survived the horror of Ginger's binge drinking. From the depths of that torture, they emerged as a closer family. It was a hard-fought battle.

Topaz often remembers the counselor at Alcoholic Anonymous who guided her mother to sobriety. In her heart she said thank you many times to the man who saved her mother's life. In counseling her mother, this gentle man brought the whole family closer together. They sustained this closeness for all their remaining years of life. It still exists, proving that love is eternal.

Through her hard work Ginger helped Papa Lebni buy a house. "This house is for everybody," Papa Lebni told Ginger. "That way you and Hathor and the children will always have someplace to stay."

One night when Lebni was somewhere beyond 70, he went into Ginger's bedroom. "Baby I want you to remember this house is for everybody. Don't sell it, and don't borrow no money against it," he told his confidante. Ginger looked at her Papa and promised, "Alright I won't Papa."

Lebni went to the back room in the house; it was his room. It was separate from Mama Hathor's room. He had a heart attack. Ginger heard him fall down, and rushed to his side. She called an ambulance. Lebni died on the way to the hospital. He was a man who did not believe in doctors anyway. He pulled his own teeth with a wrench.

By this time, Mama Hathor had converted to Catholicism. She insisted on a church funeral at Black Water Baptist Church. It seemed strange to Topaz, that Papa Lebni was having a church funeral. She didn't dwell on it too much; they were all sad. Papa was their rock. Living without him seemed surreal. Papa Lebni had not been inside a church that Topaz could recall.

Ginger arranged her father's funeral, as her mother wanted it. The service was held at Black Water Baptist Church on January 7, 1965. It was one of the coldest days in Mississippi history. The ground was frozen so hard that it was not clear whether a grave could be dug.

The preacher finished his eulogy and waited for the church people to file by and see Lebni lying in his casket, with the pin-striped wool suit he always wore, a new white shirt, and the infamous "strang around his neck."

When the casket was rolled over to Mama Hathor to see her husband for the last time on this earth, she cried publicly as only a widow who had been married for more than 60 years could do. The funeral attendants rolled the casket back to its place in front of the church. It was closed, and the service was completed.

Topaz felt a deep sadness that she had not felt before. To witness the sorrowfulness of her mother and the mournfulness of her grandmother touched her soul in a way no other life challenges had brought forth. Topaz wondered what her family would do without Papa. She did not know and had no way of answering the questions that came to her young mind.

It was during this downhearted wondering that the grave digger came into the church through the side entrance. "They forgot to bring the pine box," he announced. The pine box was what would be used to place the coffin in before it was lowered into the ground. "Somebody is gone to get it. It's gonna be at least an hour 'fo we ready to bury," the old man in overalls reported.

There was nothing to do but wait. It was too cold to go outside. Everyone knew the long drive back to Meridian; down Highway 39 south was a curvy and treacherous drive.

Slowly, people began to talk and visit as they were waiting. The family knew that Mrs. Hathor Ramah was not leaving until she saw that Lebni was resting in his grave.

In the midst of the commotion, five men walked through the side entrance of the church. A hushed tone fell over the small church, as the men walked toward Hathor. All the men looked like Lebni. They were stocky brown-skinned men, with bald heads.

As it turned out it was one of Lebni's brothers that he had not seen in more than 20 years, and his four sons. They lost touch when Lebni's brother moved from Mississippi to Texas to live with one of his sons. Since they could not read or write, and there were few telephones in those days, they lost touch with each other. They had driven from Huston, Texas to attend the funeral. It was not clear how they heard about Lebni's passing. The casket was reopened for them to view the body.

By the time the funeral home staff returned with the pine box, there was a major family reunion going on in Black Water Baptist Church. The cold ground had yielded to the firm touch of the grave-digger. Lebni Ramah was laid to rest without any further delay.

Everybody thought that Hathor would not live much longer. But she was a determined woman. It was not her time yet. Even though she was losing her sight to glaucoma, she carried on in her same simple country ways. She stayed home, cleaned, and cooked until she literally could not see how to get to the kitchen. She watched over Ginger's growing children with the same dedication that she had given to Ginger. Hathor had the lifelong habit of going to bed early and getting up early. "The early bird gets the worm," she believed.

Hathor Brown lived another 25 years. When she got too old to see after the house, Ginger went and got her birth mother, Lula Bell, to come and help take care of Mama Hathor. Lula Bell, who had recovered from drinking, was as clean as a whistle.

Lula Bell, who was more outgoing and younger than Mama Hathor, appreciated the opportunity to be of some service to the daughter she had abandoned.

Topaz felt lucky. She had two grandmothers who were like night and day. Mama Hathor was a churchgoing woman. Mama Lula Bell was a curious worldly woman, who loved people and fun.

Mama Hathor bought a plot in Black Water Cemetery for her burial. Since her conversion to Catholicism, and after the onset of complete blindness, a priest came once a week to give her holy communion. When a small goiter on the right side of her neck began to grow and choke the breath out of her, she resigned herself to meet her Maker.

The Requiem Mass said in her honor was simple and dignified. When Topaz got up to say a few words over Mama Hathor's body, she could only do what Mrs. Hathor Brown Ramah had taught her.

"Now I Lay Me Down to Sleep.
I Pray the Lord my Soul to Keep.
If I Die Before I Wake.
I Pray the Lord my Soul to Take."

Later generations would relate their family legacy to their young ones. Topaz would share this story with students she taught all over America. Hathor Brown and Lebni Ramah established through their union and marriage a tradition of Mississippi country love.

In their everyday humble lives, they taught their children and grandchildren the treasured Afro-centric values of love and commitment to the Supreme Being, family, friends, community, nation, and the world.

From their place on the planet earth, in rural Mississippi, these two souls touched many people in the world with the message of love. Their children, grandchildren, and great grandchildren are testament to their country love legacy.

Artist pencil drawing of Ginger.

2

Stolen Moments Lost Innocence!

By Furahaa Saba

Topaz grew up in a Black community. She was the daughter of Ginger Brown and Redmond Chaney. Topaz' complexion inherited the red undertone of her mother's color and the brown outer tone of her father. Her Hazel brown eyes were part of the heritage of the mixture of her natural born grandmother Lula Bell, who was mixed with Black and Native American blood. This happened because of the survival of the Native Americans, who lived in Kemper County and who did not yield to the Trail of Tears. Many of the Native Americans hid out in the woods to avoid being

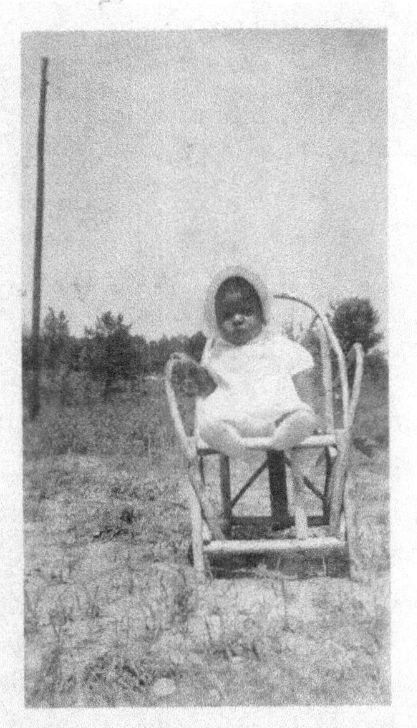

Picture of Topaz before her innocence was taken away.

captured. They lived with the Black people, who were enslaved, to survive.

Topaz didn't know much about her father Redmond Chaney. He was married to someone else. From him, she inherited a round face and a love of music. Her mother said he played the saxophone. Topaz never heard or saw him play.

Topaz had only seen her father a few times. She did know he was her father, and that he brought her a fancy red coat, when she was about 2 years old. It had fur around the collar. Topaz loved that coat. Later he bought her a pair of black patent leather shoes. Also, she had a vague recollection of a white dress with lace around the collar and sleeves.

Redmond Chaney's wife did not like the fact that he had an affair with Ginger. Topaz was the proof that Ginger and Redmond had sexual intercourse. Redmond did not visit often. He didn't stay long when he did visit.

Years later Ginger took Topaz to the mountain where she was conceived. She explained that Redmond was not active in her life. He loved her. "His wife could not have children. He cried like a baby when you were born," Ginger told Topaz.

Ginger explained these things to Topaz to try to ease some of the pain the child felt from not having a consistent relationship with her father.

The most distinct memory Topaz had of Redmond Chaney was the day he came to visit her to tell her he was leaving. He was moving to someplace called Cleveland up North. He brought her a big purple tricycle. Topaz can still see herself sitting in the yard on the big purple tricycle, while her father's black car faded into the distance on the County Home Road headed North.

Topaz sat on the tricycle an unhappy child. Mama Hathor watched the child from a distance. She let the child have a few minutes to herself. Slowly, she walked up to Topaz, and put her arm around the little girl's shoulders. She pulled her close to her body. They snuggled together for a few minutes. Mama Hathor coaxed the child off the big purple tricycle. She helped her roll it on the front porch.

*Image of the tricycle of Topaz's that
her father gave her.*

"Come on in," she beckoned the child. "I got a teacake for you," she promised. She gave Topaz a teacake from the batch she had baked that morning, along with a cool glass of water from the well.

Soon, they laid down for their afternoon nap. They were both tired. The morning had been very emotional. They laid, as they always did, side by side on Mama Hathor's bed.

That day was the beginning of the seed of abandonment Topaz felt in relation to her father. She was happy to be lying next to Mama Hathor. Their world was quiet and peaceful once again.

The house on the County Home Road was the first home Topaz could remember. Mama Hathor told her they lived in the Pecan Orchard before they moved to this house. Topaz did not remember the Pecan Orchard. She only knew what Mama Hathor told her about it.

Mama Hathor told Topaz, "Me and Ginger was working at Henderson's Grill. One day Papa Lebni came home and found you by yourself. You was only a few months old. The baby sitter, we had hired, had left you. Lebni found you dirty and crying. He cleaned you up and fed you. When me and Ginger come home he made it clear, 'One of ya'll gonna have to stay here and take care of this baby. If ya'll can't do that you may as well wash her on down Sawashee Creek.' Me and Ginger agreed. She would work at the café, and I would stay home to take care of you."

One morning the sounds of loud machines and lots of men talking raided their quiet world. The County Home Road was a bright red dirt road. Topaz was about 3 when her world was shattered. Both Topaz and her grandmother Hathor were surprised, when they heard the mixture of machines and people. They tiptoed to the front window to see what was going on.

The Black children in black-and-white-striped pants and shirts were held together by a chain. "It's a chain gang," Mama Hathor explained. "Them boys is from the jail. They chained together so they won't run away."

Seeing the question on the child's face, Mama Hathor explained. "Jail is where people go when they do bad thangs. These men have been brought out here to work on the road. It's part of what they have to do because they done wrong. They did things like take money from other people or hurt somebody with a knife or gun."

Black youth on a chain gang.

Topaz's hazel brown eyes grew wider. They did not have a television or a radio. In fact, they did not have any electricity. They got up by the light of a lamp and went to bed when the sun went down. Mama Hathor cooked on a wooden stove that Papa Lebni gathered wood for and made a fire before he left for work. Topaz's mother Ginger lit the kerosene lamps sometimes if they needed light in the evening, when she got home from the restaurant where she worked.

The young boys working on the chain gang were using tools to dig into the bright red dirt. The boys wore black-and-white pin-striped pants and shirt. Topaz did not know the word for "a White man," but he looked different from the children with the pickaxes who were chopping holes in the dirt road. The different-looking man on the horse rode up and down the line of male children working and singing as they chopped.

To be so young and witness this affected Topaz. She was terrified of going to jail. She did not want to be around people who went to jail. That image of a chain gang and the White man riding the horse and screaming at the children was a memory she buried right away. She never looked at the chain gang again, while they worked on the County Home Road.

Because she lived in an all-Black world, when someone White came around, she was keenly aware of how different Mama Hathor behaved. The two White men Topaz saw at an early age were doing things that made her feel uncomfortable. The White man on the horse bossing the chain gang talked to the children in a mean way.

The White man who knocked on their door made Mama Hathor speak in a forceful manner that Topaz had never heard. "**Who is it?**"—she asked one day when someone knocked on the front door.

It was strange because Mama Hathor and Topaz were taking a nap after doing their morning chores, breakfast, working in the garden, and having dinner, their noon meal of greens, peas, and cornbread. They had a little meat, but not much. Mostly, they ate vegetables.

"Don't fill up on that meat," Mama Hathor told the young girl. "Eat them greens, peas, and corn bread."

Very few people came to visit them. And whoever came, a relative or friend of Mama Hathor's, always came to the backdoor.

Since they lived in a segregated community, everyone who came to visit looked like them. They were the same color, only different shades of Black.

This all happened before Topaz started school. It was before she was 4 years old. Topaz heard a few grownups talking about what the "White" people did that was wrong. Because she had seen the mean White man on the horse talking bad to the Black children on the chain gang, Topaz figured out the White people were not as nice as the Black people she was around.

Topaz could sense the fear the Black people had of the White people they talked about.

She did not understand all they were saying, but she knew something was not right.

The terror that covered their world in terms of race, class, and gender was an intricate part of the daily lives of Black people. But they did not discuss these issues in political terms. They lived as if this way of life was a given, almost like it was God's will. They were simply a community of people trying to eke out a living on the lush red land, menial jobs, and small business ventures. They knew what hard times were, but they were proud of how far they had come. They were far more concerned about having a roof over their heads, enough food for winter, and praying for a better day than discussing current events.

All of Topaz's family members were descendants of enslaved people, sharecroppers, and menial laborers. They were people who had to understand the survival codes of "White Only" and "Colored." The restrictions of separate neighborhoods, churches, schools, medical shops, and shopping facilities were strictly enforced and encoded in legal and cultural structures.

It was a time before the emergence of mass media, and Topaz only knew what she saw and heard from the Black people around her. Black children were protected by their elders as much as they could from the ugliness of segregation. It was an era when children were "seen and not heard" and were expected to follow the rules of the community. Education for children was seen as a key ingredient in the improvement of the individual and was a community development process. "We watching you," adults in the community would remind children, whether the children were their own or one of the neighbors'.

One day Topaz and Mama Hathor were interrupted in their afternoon nap. Naps were a part of their daily ritual after they finished the morning chores. Their days were busy cleaning, washing, cooking, tending the garden, feeding chickens, carrying slop to their only pig, milking Betsy (the cow), churning milk, making soap, or patching quilts. Whatever needed to be done around the house was Mama Hathor's responsibility. In time, it became Topaz's duty to help her grandmother.

Mama Hathor was a great person to support. She knew how to show Topaz what to do without demanding. She was gentle in her directions. It was a skill that many would be managers could learn from.

On this particular hot Mississippi afternoon, Topaz and her grandmother heard a peculiar noise, before they were about to doze off for their well-earned nap. It was the sound of a car. A very strange thing. Not many people drove cars. Most of the Black people used a horse and wagon for trips to town.

When they heard the sound of a motor, it was weird to hear the quiet of this country community disturbed. It was also strange to hear a motor pulling into the unkept dirt- and grass-filled driveway in front of the Ramah house.

Mama Hathor laid as quiet as a mouse. She placed her caramel-colored index finger over her finely shaped thin lips signaling the child to be still and, most of all, be quiet. The old woman and the young girl listened intently as the motor was shut off. The footsteps creaked on the worn wood steps of the front porch. "Go see who it is," Mama Hathor directed Topaz in her most hushed tone.

Topaz tiptoed over to the side of the window. The peep was stealthy quick and astute. Mama Hathor had taught her how to look out to see who was at the door, with the least bit of motion. There were some days when Mama Hathor didn't want to be bothered.

"It's a big man," the child reported. "Is he White or Colored?"—the senior woman inquired in a tense whisper. The 3-year-old girl looked again. The big man was wearing a red plaid shirt and khaki pants, which were held up by wide brown suspenders. The smell from the deep brown chewed-up cigar he was smoking was seeping through the window. "He's White," the tiny little girl answered in a trembling voice.

The man knocked on the ancient wooden slab door. Initially standing as a stiff-locked doorknob, Topaz escaped across the room to her place beside Mama Hathor. Crawling over Mama Hathor's slim frame to her side of the bed, it was an intense feeling of fear to note Mama Hathor had not moved. Once the scared little girl was settled, Mama Hathor asked in a stronger voice than Topaz had ever heard her use, **"Who is it?"**

"It's Mr. Dickman, Hathor," he said. "I brought some things from up at the store, you might want to buy. It might save you the trip of walking up there," he drawled.

"Yas suh, have a seat on the porch," Mama Hathor breathed more comfortably. "I'll come out and look," the relieved woman said slowly rising from her resting position. She took her time getting up and putting on her shoes. She was already wearing her A-lined, hand-sown print housedress. Following her lead topaz strapped on white sandals that matched the store-bought pink-and-white-checked sundress she wore.

When they got to the porch, they sat in the swing. Mr. Dickman sat in a straight-back chair close to the window. Mama Hathor and Topaz swung back and forth in easy motion as he talked about what he had to sell.

"I got vanilla flavor for baking them cakes you do so well. I got some dresses, just lots of different things. Go out there and look. See if you want somethin'. Yo' credit is good with me," he slurred in a sly Southern dialect.

Dickman's was the closest store to the Ramah house. Sometimes Mama Hathor and Topaz would walk up there to get flour, meal, sugar, and Mama Hathor's favorite treat, "Tub Rose Snuff." Topaz would watch as Mama Hathor took a pinch of the dark brown powder, and placed it between her bottom lip, and her teeth. Soon she would be using a jar to spit out the liquid that formed in her mouth.

Mama Hathor bought things from Dickman's store on credit. This was contrary to Papa Lebni's rules. Papa Lebni did not believe in credit. He paid in cash or did without.

Mr. Lebni Ramah had another rule that was closely related to family security: he did not allow White people to come to our home. Mama Hatha told Topaz how Papa Lebni used to tell landowners, during his sharecropping years, "I'll work in your fields. But my wife and children do not work in your fields or house. They got enough to do at our house," Mama Hathor explained.

Mama Hathor, on the other hand, fortified her personal desire to have a few extra things in life. She marked an "x" for her name and paid as Papa Lebni and Ginger gave her money for the house. Mama Hathor was a shrewd economist with a small budget that she stretched to the very end. It was strictly a deal between Mama Hathor and the storekeeper.

Mama Hathor made her way down the red dirt embankment to the tan station wagon to see what the White man had to sell that was so important that he would come to her house. When she was in the middle of the steep incline, with her straight spine focused on balance, the nasty old White man beckoned Topaz, "Come here, I got some candy for you."

All of the child's tender senses spelled danger. The conflict was apparent. Say no and cause holy hell, or say yes and hope all would be well. She took the bait. She had never been that close to a White man before. His smell was obnoxious. She knew that both she and Mama Hathor were in danger.

Just as her tiny hand reached for the red sucker, the nasty old White man pulled Topaz's young body between his gigantic thighs. With one gesture he spun her around and placed her shapely booty smack between his legs. His gruff left hand slowly crawled beneath the white panties to her innocent vagina. The slime of his puffy dirty hands sliding on her salad bowl (this is what Mama Hathor called her private parts) was immediately buried in the child's subconscious mind. She endured what she knew was wrong, because she knew that she and Mama Hathor did not have anyone around to help them fight off the big nasty White man.

Topaz stood between his legs and looked over the pine top trees for the horizon. She felt afraid and violated. If she made a noise or resisted in any way, she knew the big White man would cause more problems for them. She did not know technically what had just happened. But she knew it was not right. No one had ever touched her like that. And Mama Hathor had already taught her that her salad bowl was only touched when she was cleaning it.

Topaz was forced in that moment to keep a secret bigger than her age. Mr. Dickman stopped rubbing and feeling on her as Mama Hathor turned around from her brief shopping venture.

Topaz moved back to her place on the swing without uttering a sound. When the mammoth redneck man offered the candy to the little girl again, she simply shook her head no. That was a moment in childhood when survival required the aching of a grown woman.

Who could she tell? What could she do?

If she told Mama Hathor they would have been forced to defend their lives in the backwoods of Mississippi against a White man. There was no one to help them. No telling what kind of weapon Mr. Dickman had in his giant-sized pockets or car. What if he decided to force himself on both of them?

If the molested child told her mother, Ginger, she would be worried about them while she was working at the café. If the young girl told Papa Lebni, her grandfather, he would hunt Mr. Dickman down to shoot him with the shotgun he kept leaning against the wall in the backroom.

Topaz had seen with her own eyes how the Black people were treated on the chain gang.

She heard the prison guard torture the Black prisoners with insults, "Nigger that hole ain't deep enough." She could not stand the idea of risking her grandfather's freedom or life. Topaz' father had already left to go north to live in Cleveland, Ohio. Every once in a while, he sent a letter, which Ginger read to Topaz.

As Hathor turned around, she told Mr. Dickman, "You got some nice-looking thangs, but I don't think I'll be needin' anythang today." She sat back in the swing and began to slowly sway carrying Topaz into a peaceful motion with her. Mr. Dickman dragged his heavy body on back to his car. "You come on up the store, Hathor, when you need something," he said as he slid down the dirt incline to his car.

Mama Hathor and Topaz sat in the afternoon heat, swinging and humming "Jesus Keep Me Near the Cross." They watched and listened until there was no sign of Mr. Dickman. When their nerves were sufficiently rested, they went inside to start supper.

Topaz had a moment to herself when Mama Hathor told her, "Go out to the woodpile and get some kindlin' to start the fire." Topaz took advantage of the moment to breathe deeply, and suppress, the total invasion she felt.

No one in the Ramah family ever knew what Mr. Dickman stole from Topaz that afternoon.

This was the first time Topaz was violated. She refused to let these circumstances take away her healthy sexual appetite. Topaz was never intimate with another White man. Some White men were attracted to her as an adult, but they all smelled like Mr. Dickman to her.

In the worst of circumstances, there is always a saving grace. Even though Topaz had been sexually assaulted at the tender age of 3, she intuitively knew not to let that experience cloud her whole life. She pushed the memory in the back of her mind and put on a big smile. She remained positive, outgoing, friendly, and loving throughout her life.

3

Lacy Bottom Reader

By Furahaa Saba

During the 1950s, Topaz Ramah lived with her family in Lacy Bottom, Mississippi. The small country settlement consisted of about 12 Black and several poor White families. Nestled on the outskirts of Meridian, "Queen City" of Mississippi, the houses sat in the midst of heavily wooded land next to a dried-up ditch on Highway 39 North.

During the summer months, Topaz would get up before everyone in her house. She couldn't wait to get to the back steps so she could watch Cousin Adora, who was the Lacy Bottom Reader.

As she heard the rooster down the road crow, she would slip out of bed and into her robe and slippers. Topaz always wore slippers, because chickens ran loose in the yard, and Topaz did not like stepping in their waste.

Topaz cherished the early-morning quiet. She could sit on the steps and smell the aroma of pine trees mixed with fresh air. Most of all, the curious child loved seeing who was coming to visit Cousin Adora early in the morning before the neighborhood was fully awake.

Cousin Adora was the Lacy Bottom Reader. A reader is a person in the community who uses various instruments like cards, a crystal

Land kept the people alive.

ball, tea leaves, or coffee grinds to predict the future. A reader is a person whose business is to provide hope and warnings about life's twists and turns to believers.

Cousin Adora was a tall, blackberry-hued woman. She swayed like a bush on a warm Southern afternoon when she moved. She never hurried. Most of the time her head was covered with a red or blue polka dot head rag. Only her jet-black bangs pressed to her forehead would extend slightly from the kerchief she wore. The scarf was tied neatly at the nape of her neck. Cousin Adora had a flair for color; her A-Lined floral print dresses were bright and neatly pressed. She adorned whatever dress she was wearing with a starched, sometimes clashing print apron which covered her slightly protruding stomach. The perfectly tied bow at the back of the apron accented her flat behind. She was a woman who stood back in her legs. This means

Cousin Adora was a wise woman with a sweet spirit.

the weight was placed on the heals of her feet as opposed to being evenly distributed.

Moving through the sleeping house, Topaz was always reminded of the fact that her Grandfather, Lebni, had built the house with his own hands, using the scraps of metal and tin he collected with his mule and wagon. While working on his day job as a pulpwood logger, he would scout places that had discarded materials he could use to build his family a home. When the truck dropped him off after a full day of work, he would hitch up the mule and wagon to fetch the treasures he had spotted. There were mixed-matched materials and places where the wind came into the house. Papa Lebni was proud of the fact that he was on his own land. After having been abandoned by his parents, being a sharecropper and pulpwood logger most of his life, he beamed at his ownership. It took a long time to save the $65.00 to buy the land and a few years to build the house bit by bit.

Cousin Adora fascinated Topaz because she was one of the few people Grandmother Hathor allowed to visit inside the Ramah home. Mama Hathor liked people, but she believed, "Handle them with a long-handled spoon." Topaz had been taught to become invisible when the women visited. "Chillun' ain't got no business tending to grown folks' business," Mama Hathor insisted.

Whenever Cousin Adora came over for a visit, Topaz did not have to be told to go to the back steps and sit quietly until they were finished.

She made sure to get water or whatever she needed before she left. There was no such thing as running in and out of the house while adults were talking.

Often Topaz eavesdropped on what she could hear. Usually Cousin Adora came to complain about Cousin Jacob, her husband. Mama Hathor never discussed her personal business.

Cousin Jacob was a dark pecan-colored man. He was taller than Cousin Adora by a head. His appearance was rumpled compared to hers. His dark work pants and shirt were covered with smatterings of grease. He had a habit of pushing his baseball cap back to scratch his receding hair line. Cousin Jacob drove a raggedy old brown pickup truck. He hauled everything from children to trash. Most people snickered at the rickety truck, until they needed a ride. Cousin Jacob would do whatever he could to help anyone.

Cousin Adora was not concerned about the many people Cousin Jacob helped. But she told mama Hathor, "Them tacky women Jacob is layin' 'round with is gettin' on my nerves. He came tippin' in this mornin' about 7 a.m. He threw up his hands and just told me to do whatever I wanted to do to him."

"Just shoot me or cut me," the heartbroken woman waved her hands in the air mimicking Cousin Jacob's motions.

Mama Hathor responded, "Awh, that's a shame."

It was common to hear fights in Lacy Bottom between husbands and wives about adultery. Mama Hathor considered her role as a community elder to be one of setting a good example. She understood the turmoil that young love presented. But she held to the notion that older people should have learned how to be with each other.

Although Cousin Adora was upset about the cheating behavior of her husband, she was no saint. From the little girl's listening place, she heard other women talk about Cousin Adora sleeping with the preacher, Reverend People, of the Community Baptist Church.

One morning Topaz saw a woman walking through the woods carrying a thin white coffee cup. Sitting in her favorite viewing place, Topaz could see the mysterious woman creeping through the brush on a well-used path to Cousin Adora's backdoor. The woman knocked quietly. It was obvious that she did not want to disturb the entire household. "Miss Adora," she called in a loud whisper. Cousin Jacob probably heard the woman, but he did not answer.

Cousin Adora came to the backdoor and stood on the inside of the screen door in full regalia. She smiled as she stepped out the door. The experienced woman asked, "How can I help you?"

Picture of coffee cup that was used for readings.

"I brought the grinds from the first cup of coffee of the morning. I need to know what they say," the thin-framed woman requested humbly.

Cousin Adora looked the woman over carefully. "I can tell you the truth if you can stand it."

She took the woman's coffee cup. She shifted the grinds in all four directions, north, south, east, west. Cousin Adora Looked into the woman's eyes, "Honey, you need to be true to you. You know the truth. Do I have to tell you he is cheating on himself, you and ya'lls chillen?"—she asked.

Cousin Adora spread the coffee grinds in the yard, before she gave the cup back to the woman, who took the cup with down-thrust eyes. "Maybe I need a tea leaf reading," she suggested.

"Wait for a week or so," Cousin Adora responded. "A tea reading is a serious thing. Use only lobelia tea leaves. It will be ready to gather in a few more days. Steep the leaves the night before and drink a cup. Bring the leaves early in the morning before you speak to anyone."

Topaz was on pins and needles all through the week. She made sure to get up extra early everyday so she would not miss the reading of the tea leaves. Several other women came for coffee grind readings throughout the week. But the small mysterious woman did not come back for two weeks. When she did come, Topaz could see from her hidden place on her back steps, large blue and black bruises on the woman's brown face and arms.

"He beat me again," she told Cousin Adora, as she carefully handed her the tea cup. Both women sat on the glider of the back porch. "Lets start with a prayer," Cousin Adora insisted. They bowed their heads in silent prayer. Topaz sensed that each woman's prayer was different. Cousin Adora was praying for inspiration. The mysterious woman was praying for the love of her man.

When they finished the silent prayer, Cousin Adora stood up with the tea cup and walked to the edge of the porch facing the sun. She turned the cup in a complete clockwise circle. She held the cup up toward the universal blue sky. "God Bless the reading of your word," she prayed.

Turning back to the woman anxiously waiting on the glider, she began. "Honey, you know God don't make no mistakes. His way is not always easy or what we want. But, to tell you the truth, these tea leaves say that man is either gonna leave you or kill you. You must let him go. Help him to leave. Don't cling on to him. He don't mean you no good," Cousin Adora advised.

"But, how I'm gonna feed my childrin? I don't have no money, no job, no 'perience 'cept working in the fields."

"Do what you have to do. Go back to the fields. It'll be enough to keep a roof over ya'lls heads and food on the table. You have to ask yo'self the bigger question, 'what will happen to my chillen if he beats me to death?'"

Handing the delicate tea cup back to the distraught woman, Cousin Adora gave the woman the best advice she knew, "God will take of y'all."

The woman took the cup with trembling hands. She reached in her apron pocket and gave Cousin Adora some change before she headed back through the woods. Her heavy and hesitant footsteps foretold the hard labor that lay before her.

Topaz watched Cousin Adora all summer. She saw many women come through the woods seeking a reading. But she never saw the mysterious woman with the beaten body again.

Once school started Topaz didn't have time to sit on the back steps early in the morning. She would often peep out the window and see a woman in pain headed toward Cousin Adora's backdoor. She didn't hear Cousin Adora complain about Cousin Jacob again. The following year Topaz's family moved out of Lacy Bottom to Meridian. Topaz never saw Cousin Adora again.

Still, Cousin Adora made a deep impact on Topaz. She touched her soul. Topaz learned from paying attention to Cousin Adora that there are many ways of solving problems. Through this experience she learned at an early age to connect with the elements of nature to solve human problems. She became a lifelong lover of different teas. She liked the smell of coffee but could not tolerate the caffeine. So she kept tasting and liking teas.

From sitting on the back steps in Lacy Bottom and watching Cousin Adora and the women who came to see her, Topaz developed an interest in divination at an early age. She became interested in Astrology, Tarot Cards, Cartouche, an Egyptian Card divination system as well as the Native American Medicine Cards. She loved the world they took her into because it was not just an ordinary answer; those systems opened new worlds of thought to her. As she grew older she would use any one of these systems and others to examine her own life.

Topaz's questions were usually about a man, money, a job, or some business venture. The symbols carried in such art forms were pleasing to Topaz's mind because they expanded her considerations beyond the realm of logic. It was a world she loved learning. These experiences helped Topaz connect to the Divine Feminine within her. It was a world where she could connect with her own soul.

She was not sure if she was accurately interpreting the information, but she treasured the idea of having the tools to travel beyond the limitations of her Black Catholic background, exploring the realm of life's mysteries.

4

Passage into White Hands!

Grandmother Hathor told Topaz the truth of her experience living in Mississippi as a Black woman. "I was born on April 1, 1892 in what folks called 'Bloody' Kemper County."

It was a miracle that Mama Hathor knew her birthdate. Many Black people born during that historical era did not have any idea about their date of birth. Topaz never knew how Mama Hathor knew. It was a fact passed on in the Ramah family and celebrated as long as a Ramah was alive.

It was even more fascinating when Topaz realized her grandmother had only finished the second grade. She could not read most things. She knew enough to pass on the history she remembered to her granddaughter. "You have to know yo' folks," she told the child.

"My mother's mother, Ma Kate, was a slave. On Sunday evenings she used to gather us chulllin' around in the front yard. She would tell us how hard it was to be a slave. 'We worked in the fields from sunup to sundown. We just had a little to eat. It was hard work. We bent down over the cotton, and the sun was beatin' down on us. Mostly we et scraps of meat and bread left over from Massa's house. Massa wouldn't even let us have a garden to raise food. We slept on straw and hard floors. Ma' Kate use to tell us chillin," Grandmother Hathor told Topaz.

Grandma Hathor would occasionally tell Topaz about her family history during their nap time, which was after dinner, the noon meal. "I'm tellin' you about these things so you can know that life can be hard. But, you don't have to let it get you down," she would say with a peaceful gaze. As the old song goes, "Trouble don't last always."

On some days Mama Hathor would talk about herself. The old woman wanted the young girl to know her background.

The Ramah family lived a calm rural life. As with many people in the South, sometimes a person's name was not clear. For example, how the Ramah's became Ramah's has been lost in history. Ramah, according to the Hebrew Bible, was the name of a city in Ancient Israel. It was not clear how the name became associated with the Ramah family. Some family members speculated that some of the elders had been the property of some Ramah's. But no one knew for sure.

Lebni in the Bible means white. How Lebni Ramah got that name, if it was his real name, was not known. It was odd because Lebni means white, or it could refer to a cheese that is made from yogurt. It was speculated that some plantation owner had given Lebni that name or misunderstood his real name and just called him Lebni.

Lebni Ramah was the head of the Ramah household. The Ramah's, like many Black families, had endured some hard times.

Mama Hathor was a special blessing to the Ramah family. "Ya'll gonna miss me when I 'm dead and gone," she used to tell them in moments of frustration. An agreement between Ginger, the child's mother, and Mama Hathor caused this divine intervention into Topaz's life. Ginger and Hathor worked as waitresses at a Black-owned café in the flourishing Black business district of Meridian, Mississippi, for several years before Topaz was born.

One day, shortly after her birth in December 1948, Papa Lebni, came home early. He decided to pick Topaz up from the babysitter's house. He walked through the pecan orchard to get her. "You was nasty and crying. The babysitter had left you with a heap of otha chillum. No grown people were at the house. Lebni brough you to our house, cleaned you up and fed you. When yo' mama and me got home from work," Lebni laid down the law. Hathor told Topaz that Lebni insisted, "One of ya'll got to stay here and take care of dis baby. If you ain't gonna do that, you may as well wash her down Sawashi creek," Mama Hathor told Topaz when she was old enough to understand.

Ginger and Hathor made an agreement that day. Since Ginger was the youngest, and had the greatest earning potential, she would keep the job in the café, while Grandmother Hathor stayed home to watch over Topaz.

Mama Hathor assumed her duties as primary caregiver. She established a routine that would prepare Topaz for life, while making sure her charge met her standards for being in her presence. "I don't care if yo' head gets as clean as the palm of my hand, you will mind me," the aging woman firmly and consistently reminded the hard-headed child. The child had to fit into the senior woman's nerve patterns, while crawling toward adulthood.

Mrs. Hathor Brown Ramah considered education to be the best route for Topaz's escape to freedom. In fact, the whole family and community operated on the principle of educating children. In the simplest manner, considerable effort was directed toward getting ready for school, like establishing a routine of getting up early and going to bed early. "Git sumin in yo' head. Nobody can take that away from you," Papa Lebni preached every time the opportunity arose.

Finally, the first day of kindergarten , September 1952 came into view. Topaz's mother, Ginger, had changed jobs to work at an exclusive "For Whites Only" restaurant, where she could make more money. She waited on tables, walked on concrete floors until her feet became tender with corns and bunions, to be sure the child had everything needed for life in general and school in particular.

As mother and daughter got into the old black Chevy, for the drive to St. Jame's Black Catholic school, Ginger looked over and smiled at Topaz, with pride. Topaz had the mandatory blue and white pleated uniform skirt with a white blouse. Mama Hathor had neatly pressed the skirt and blouse with a small black iron heated on the wooden stove. Her white underwear and socks were bright and new. The Buster Brown black and white oxfords were hard on her feet but bearable. A neighbor lady had stretched the little sandy brown hair Topaz had with a hot straightening comb. Ginger managed to pull together four short plaits. She looked her 4-year-old daughter over for a final inspection as they sat in the car. She smiled. Topaz returned her mother's smile feeling happy she was making her mother proud.

Ginger cranked up the old black car, ignoring the pain piercing through her feet as she pushed the clutch in with her right foot and braked with her aching left foot. She backed out onto the County Home Road. On the way to school, Ginger took the opportunity to reiterate her expectations. She talked while driving, "You be a good girl and learn all you can. I quit school in the sixth grade and let me tell you it's hard."

Ginger stopped talking to let Topaz take in the new sights. She slowed the car as they approached the school. Finally, they stopped in front of a small, gray, wooden-frame building. Lots of little Black children were playing in the fenced yard. Ginger leaned over to hug Topaz and kiss her goodbye. The little girl opened the car door and saw a pale-skinned woman in a long black dress with beads hanging from the side, coming toward her. The pale woman's head was covered with a long black veil, trimmed with starched white headgear. Topaz screamed and retreated back into the car crawling toward her mother. She had only seen a few White men. She had never seen a White woman. Nor had she seen a Catholic nun at Blackwater Baptist Church, the only church she had attended before that day.

Sister Mary Charity spoke in a heavy German accent. She was a part of the generation of Catholics who immigrated to America to escape the tortures of Hitler. She stretched her hand toward Topaz, "Come I will not harm you," she promised.

Topaz sucked in her breath and took Sister Mary Charity's outstretched hand. The Catholic German nun slowly walked Topaz into the school building. The child discovered that beneath the pale skin, funny accent, and mysterious clothes was a woman dedicated to saving souls through the medium of reading, writing, and arithmetic.

Topaz became a teacher on the first day of kindergarten. After school when she returned home to Grandmother Hathor, the old woman asked, "What did you learn today?" Everyday after that, all the way through elementary school, Grandmother Hathor increased her second-grade education by insisting that the child answer the question, "What did you learn today?" Grandmother Hathor gave Topaz the gift of attentive listening and genuine questions. This instilled in the child the skill of explaining academic concepts in everyday terms.

Becoming educated was not easy for Topaz. She had to battle the conflict between what was in the books and the reality of the Black world in which she lived. She also had to struggle to separate the information from the persuasive intent of Catholicism. The education, while being a tool for mind expansion, was also the bitter pill that contributed to Topaz's lack of knowledge of herself and her people. Once she discovered this grievous error, she started on her personal search for truth.

The advantage of a Catholic education for Topaz was that she mastered the basics of learning reading and writing. These tools helped her read and write and to be able to find information. She had a lifelong interest in learning new things. She was not so good at the mathematics they taught, but she did learn in time to appreciate the value of counting.

More than the school itself, through her exposure to Catholicism, Topaz learned that not all White people are mean. She learned how to be with people of a different cultural background than her own.

In spite of the battle Topaz fought with Catholicism, she valued the discipline she learned in spiritual practices. She appreciated going to mass, saying the Latin prayers, the different postures for praying.

After graduating from a Catholic college in 1970, Topaz was very upset that she had a Catholic education from kindergarten through a Bachelor of Arts degree. With all her education, she had very little information about her Black cultural background. This lack of knowledge caused Topaz to withdraw from her Catholic beliefs and practices. She was mad that more information about Black culture had not been included in her education.

She embarked on a journey of learning about Black culture, which she continues today. No matter how disappointed she was in her discovery of Catholic conflicts, she always respected and valued the education she received from her Catholic schools, which gave her the tools to read, research, and explore every learning experience she encountered. Topaz had to admit that her Catholic education taught her the discipline of learning. Most of all, Topaz learned to think an issue through.

Topaz often reflected on the advice her grandfather, Papa Lebni, had planted in her heart, "Git some 'em in yo' head. That's some'em nobody can take from you."

Topaz seemed rebellious in a lot of ways, culturally, religiously, politically, and so forth, but she was deeply grateful that she had followed her grandfather's advice.

Topaz concluded for her life, "I am happy that I learned to mix with all kinds of people. Knowing my Black roots helps me bring a unique perspective to each experience."

5

The Coming-Out of Mr. Little's Spirit

Mr. John Little lived quietly with his wife Mrs. Cindy Lou, across the ditch from my family in Lacy Bottom, Mississippi. This mostly Black settlement was at the foot of the Shelly Waddell Hills on the outskirts of Meridian, Mississippi. Lacy

Mr. Little's house was scary looking, but it was safe during storms.

Bottom was a heavily wooded community located in the heart of east Mississippi and west central Alabama.

Most of the Black people who lived in this community worked in the fields of nearby farmers. Flatbed trucks would come to Lacy Bottom in the morning to pick up adults and children for the hot, rough ride to work in the seasonal crops of cotton, watermelon, string beans, corn, and tomatoes. Whatever the farmers were growing in a season, the Black people harvested.

Some of the Black women of Lacy Bottom worked in the homes of White women as maids, babysitters, and cooks. Some of the Black men worked as drivers, gardeners, and pulpwood choppers. Most of the Black people had little money and menial jobs, trying to make a better way of life for themselves and their children. Black folks prided themselves on how far they had come when they could get a plot of land in Lacy Bottom, Mississippi.

My grandfather built our four-room house with his own hands from scraps of wood he collected around town with his horse and buggy. He had worked to end his sharecropping debt and saved to provide a home for his family to the best of his ability.

The Black people of Lacy Bottom were fancy in their hearts. In the homes and restaurants where they worked, they saw how glamorous white people lived and wined and dined. Because of this, they tried to replicate this fanciness to the best of their ability in their own homes.

Five wooden four-room houses with tin roofs stood gracefully among pine, pecan, and plum trees laced with honey suckle and blackberry bushes in the heart of Lacy Bottom. Intricately decorated outhouses made of scrap wood with ribbed tin roofs were painted shades of cheap blue, yellow, and brown paint. The sparkling clean out-houses lined the east side of the Lacy Bottom's dried-up ditch.

Many people gathered fruits like pears, plums, figs, blackberries, and strawberries from the surrounding grounds for preserving. Some people collected herbs like sassafras, peppermint, spearmint, mullein fever grass, chamomile, and white oak bark for making medicines. While there was an easygoing country lifestyle, there was an implicit roughness in this Mississippi existence.

You could hear the hard living from the Chicken Shack, the neighborhood juke joint. The Chicken Shack sat in the forest and rang out the sounds of Mississippi blues all day long, when it was open. The bass continually put out the survival beat, and the melody of the piano reminded everyone to go to church on Sunday. The heat was riving up. By the time Miss Lula Mae finished frying the chicken, it was a serious country party.

Slim Jim, the guitar player, struck a cord to ease the horror. God knows help was needed from somewhere. By the time the drummer connected the sounds to Mother Earth, all of Lacy Bottom seemed to be swaying with the wind. If a singer was in the juke joint, without fail somebody would wave a hand, cuss, shake some booty, and/or shed a tear.

The serious weekend "Wang Dang Doodle" would begin late Friday afternoon when Mr. Shelly Waddell, an old White man who lived up in the hills adjacent to Lacy Bottom, would come down from his whiskey steel in an old blue 1950s Chevrolet.

Lauderdale County, the governing seat of Lacy Bottom and its sister town, Meridian, was a dry county until the mid-1960s. It was illegal to sell, drink, or possess any type of alcohol. But no one ever stopped, arrested, or harassed old man Waddell. He would drive up to the front door of the Chicken Shack and have two of his White boy cronies unload the trunk full of illegal firewater. By the time the Black men and women had enough of what was locally called "Poot Whiskey," or Moonshine, the rage of somebody's life had to come out.

A fight was inevitable. You could hear the sash of a fist and the riff of a knife cutting through the echoes of B.B. King, Bobby Blue Bland, John Lee Hooker, or whatever blues singer was being played on the rockola, a freestanding machine that played 45 rpms.

Mr. John Little was a contrast to this environment. There were a lot of tall hedges around his house, which was sitting on the west side of Lacy Bottom's ditch. It was a big spooky-looking house, which had better-quality materials than the other homes. The speckled brown

Impression of the beekeeper who made friends with Topaz.

siding and thick shining tin roof looked more expensive than the plain wooden houses with thin tin roofs.

My two cousins, who lived next door to us, and I would watch the strange-looking house from across the ditch. We knew someone lived there, but we never saw anyone. We wondered about all those cages in the backyard. What were they? Why were they there? Why was the tin on their roof so thick and shiny? Was that siding stuff expensive? What was it like to have a screened-in back porch? What did people do in such a place?

We watched to see what questions we could answer. We would move along the ditch on our side to get a better view. Pulling the bushes back, we were trying to see in a way befitting of curious little girls. There was a flat wooden plank that served as a bridge across the waterless ditch. We were not allowed to cross the bridge.

One summer day we actually saw the back screen door open. Mr. John Little walked out. We were as quiet and still as life would allow. I was so excited, I didn't know where to look first. I took in a deep breath, focused my cat-like eyes and decided to start from the bottom up.

From the ground his black riding boots stopped at his knees. Kha-ki pants were stuffed inside the boots. The black belt he wore foretold a small frame. Wearing a long-sleeved khaki shirt, his arms were covered with some kind of net and thick padding. His slim pale hands were uncovered. He carried a long-handled net in his right hand. By the time I reached the top of his head, I had to catch my breath.

I could not see his face. The Safari hat he was wearing blocked my view because it was draped with a heavy net.

Scholars would describe us as economically poor, female adolescents growing up in segregated rural Mississippi. We did not know we were poor. We were three happy, curious little girls. Like children all over the world, we wanted to know about our neighbors.

We saw something that mid-1950s day. The automatic bulging of our eyes was as natural as the shallow breaths we took as Southern girls. The shock of it all was a part of our upbringing. We thought we had seen something from another world. Maybe we had.

We watched in frozen posture as the little White man walked steadily toward the cages. The path was worn. We were amazed as he opened the first cage. He gently pushed the long-handled net he carried in his right hand inside the cage.

We could see and hear the swarming of bees as they covered his hands and arms. Calmly, he completed his beekeeping tasks and returned inside the mysterious house.

We were so outdone we didn't know what to do. We looked at each other in wonder. Slowly, we backed up from the bushes in our best quiet step. We tipped home, speechless.

One day the little White man caught me peeping by myself. He beckoned through the hedges across the ditch for me to come over. Against all known rules, I ventured across the ditch. As soon as I stepped on the plank, I violated the core of my family's safety rules. I walked over of my own free will. He took my hand and led me on the narrow path leading to his front door.

Up close and without all his beekeeping gear, I could see he was a pale White man of small stature. His auburn-colored hair was mixed with gray. Small gold-rimmed glasses circled his clear-blue eyes. Thick eyebrows matching his hair flopped around his forehead. He was a slow-moving man.

"I have something for you to give to your grandmother," he said as we made our way toward his front porch. I guess he had been watching us too.

His wife, Mrs. Cindy Lou, was sitting in the swing on the front porch swaying back and forth in an easy motion with her bare feet. She slowed down as we approached. She said hello in a kind voice.

He followed her inside the screen door. I followed both of them inside their house. Obviously, I was in a daze.

My grandmother was in her early 50s during this era. She was a gentle but firm disciplinarian. "Your head can get as clean as the palm of my hand, but you will always do what I say," she consistently reminded me. This reality was backed up with the down-thrust-eye prediction, "Ya'll gonna miss me, when I am dead and gone."

She was our family caretaker. Everyone else worked. My survival depended on my ability to conform to her rules. Thankfully, she was a seasoned loving woman.

Grandmother did not allow me to be, "Going into other folks' houses" on our side of the ditch. All the children of Lacy Bottom inherently knew at an early age the difference between Black and White people. I had to have direct permission to go into my cousin's house. It was unthinkable to cross the bridge and go over to these White people's world.

In spite of it all, I found myself at this moment in life, walking across this bridge following a White man. I was actually allowing two White people to lead me inside their home. This violation of local cultural norms was enormous.

Mrs. Cindy Lou led her husband and me inside the house down a wide hallway. Her long ponytail seemed to be swaying in tune with her bare feet. We walked straight through the hallway. On a table with a starched white table cloth sat a brown Philco Radio. The sound of the music playing was different from the bluesy vibrations of the Chicken Shack. The soft classical sound could be heard as we entered the kitchen.

Mrs. Cindy Lou handed Mr. Little a jar without saying a word. He gave the jar to me explaining, "This is honey. My wife makes it from the bees I take care of in the backyard." As my grandmother had patiently taught me, I thanked them, while eyeing the delicious-looking treat. The honey had a golden tone, and a deep brown cone was standing erect in the middle of the Mason jar. My boundaries had been expanded far enough for one day. I thanked them again and made my way back across the bridge.

When I showed grandmother the honey, she looked at the honey, and she looked at me. Finally she opened the jar saying, "You gonna taste it first. If it kills anybody, it's going to kill you first."

I was ready to die—the honey looked so delicious. And it was. It was such a soothing, cooling experience sliding down my throat. I still smile deeply at the memory.

The next morning Mama, as we affectionately called our grandmother, went out to her garden and picked a bucket of collard greens. She washed and chopped them finely. She cooked them in a big black cast-iron pot on the wooden stove. Mama divided the collard greens and gave me half to take over to Mr. and Mrs. Little.

That was the beginning of our neighborly exchange. We sat through births, deaths, political upheavals, tornadoes, and other tragedies from that day until we moved away from Lacy Bottom.

Since that time I have traveled across many bridges of the world. I have tasted many types of foods. No one cooks better collard greens than Mama. Nothing has been sweeter than the spirit of Mr. Little's honey. For these and all the other blessings, I am deeply grateful.

6

The Flower Lady

rs. Azalea Samuels St. John survived the death of her parents, grandparents, and two husbands. These crushing life blows caused the Mississippi woman to develop a humble yet resilient personality at a tender age.

Miss Azalea, as she is affectionately called according to the Meridian, Mississippi Black culture, is the mother of six children. Twice-widowed, she ended up being a single parent for the majority of the children's upbringing. She confronted the dilemmas all single parents face: the conflict between work, time with family, and the emotional and financial strain of being alone as head of the household. The pensions she received from the deaths of her husbands were not enough to provide for the growing girls and boy. She had to work.

Azalea flowers inspired happiness in the poverty-stricken neighborhood.

Magnolia flowers are a reminder of the strict southern traditions.

The image of Miss Azalea walking up the hill of Mulberry Lane in Meridian is a portrait of a woman struggling with the weight of having cleaned an entire office building as well as a private mansion in one workday. Miss Azalea projected a wide and inviting smile, regardless of how far in hell she had been in one day. For 40 years, 5 days a week, Miss Azalea met every workday with the labor of her body. It seemed the harder she worked, the brighter her smile beamed.

Most days, Miss Azalea would be carrying a brown paper bag of groceries or other household necessities when she made her way up the hill toward her five-room home. When she reached her house she would hold on to the strong iron rail to climb the first 12 steps. After accomplishing that considerably steep task, she would stand and catch her breath before tackling the remaining six steps leading to the front porch.

The neighborhood children of Mulberry Lane heard about Miss Azalea before they met her. She was the grandmother and caretaker of Black-Eyed Susan, one of the most notorious young girls of the area. Black-Eyed Susan wasn't bad, but she was tough. She was a tall ten-year-old, who withstood beatings from Miss Azalea, and her baby-sitting teenage uncle, like a horse.

No matter how much they beat Black-Eyed Susan, she still would skip out on her household chores and homework to play ball.

Black-Eyed Susan didn't do things like stealing or hurting people. She just liked to play any kind of ball (soft ball, dodge ball, kick ball, basketball, volley ball) before she finished her assigned household chores or started homework. Regardless of the yelling and beatings she got with the leather strap, whose holes had been widened to insure sucking of the flesh, Black-Eyed Susan was still the first one outside to play ball.

Miss Azalea was doing an outstanding job raising Black-Eyed Susan as well as her own children. Miss Azalea was the mother of four daughters from her first marriage. She had one son from her second marriage.

Miss Azalea's life as an adult was different from the life she had as a child. She was an only child. Her grandparents had raised her after the early death of her parents. Having five children and one granddaughter was not a family situation she was familiar with. She had to figure out how to manage everything on her own.

Her youngest daughter, son, and Black-Eyed Susan lived at home. The older children graduated from high school and moved north to go to college and begin their own families in the late 1950s and early 1960s. They regularly sent money, clothes, and whatever else they could to support their mother and the younger children. Miss Azalea taught all the children—"We have to help each other. There is no one else to depend on."

Black-Eyed Susan was the daughter of Miss Azalea's oldest daughter, but folks in the community considered Miss Azalea as the mother of Black-Eyed Susan. Being an unwed mother was not an acceptable status during that time, for a girl who wanted to attend college. Someone in the family would take the children, care for them, while the mother completed her education.

This was Black-Eyed Susan's station in life. Her mother was completing school while her grandmother took care of her. It was generally accepted that Black-Eyed Susan would go to live with her mother one day.

Black-Eyed Susan was often left at home with her teenage uncle as her babysitter. "You better get in here and wash these baseboards," his changing masculine voice demanded. No response. A few minutes later, the whip of the leather strap penetrated the neighborhood airwaves. Black-Eyed Susan would scream for the whole world to hear. "I'm not telling you again, do these baseboards," the young man insisted.

Young people had to create their own fun, there were few manufactured toys.

Soon afterwards Black-Eyed Susan would be seen coming down the steps. She would go to a neighbor's house or just find some place to hide on Mulberry Lane.

Black-Eyed Susan was the kind of girl who just had things happen to her. One day instead of being at home doing her own chores she was at a neighbor's house helping a friend do laundry. The 1950s-style washer was the type that required removing each piece of clothing from the tub and placing it between two metal bars that looked like rolling pins. Black-Eyed Susan, a great humorist, was laughing and talking with her girlfriend and not paying attention to how close her fingers were to metal bars of the washing machine. Her hand and lower arm got caught between the metal bars up to her elbow. When the girls finally managed to unwind Black-Eyed Susan's right arm from the bars, she struck out running for home. No real damage was done to her arm, but she did stay home for a few days. It was quiet in the neighborhood. There wasn't a single ball game on Mulberry Lane until Black-Eyed Susan recovered.

Black-Eyed Susan loved to organize neighborhood ball games.

She had sat on the steps and bounced the white ball with black strips until enough children came outside to play. It was a hot, humid, Mississippi summer day. The sun was beating down rays of heat, but the children were oblivious to it. "I have to go take the clothes off the line before Mama comes home," she kept telling the children. But the game absorbed her attention.

As the day changed into evening, it was time for people to start coming home from work. Black-Eyed Susan looked down the hill and saw Miss Azalea coming up the hill. She hoodwinked one of her friends into helping her get the clothes off the clothesline before her grandmother made it up the hill. "We don't have enough time to get them in. It's too many. I hung out two lines. Help me unwind the hose. We'll wet them down," Black-Eyed Susan convinced her help-mate. "Turn the water on," she directed the draftee. Black-Eyed Susan hosed down all the clothes that had been hanging on the clothesline all day in the gleaming Mississippi summer sunshine. Like lightning they descended the steps and were back at the dodge ball game before Miss Azalea reached the top of the hill.

"Hey Miss Azalea," the children spoke to the friendly old lady. "Hey Babies. How ya'll doin'?"—she replied as she made her way home. The children stopped the dodge ball game, as a sign of respect until Miss Azalea made it up the first flight of stairs. Each child knew Miss Azalea was tired and did not want to hear any unnecessary noise. They had all been taught to respect adults.

There was something special about Miss Azalea's greeting to the children. The dozen or so boys and girls knew that Miss Azalea was going to send them uplifting thoughts. She took her time and gave a personal smile to each child. No more words were required.

After a few minutes, Miss Azalea came to the front door. "Black-Eyed Susan, why are all my clothes soaking wet?"—she demanded. "It rained Mama," the child claimed. "Come here," her grandmother sighed, mumbling under her breath so the other children would not see her complete disgust with Black-Eyed Susan.

The children knew Black-Eyed Susan had been caught in a bold lie. "You gonna get a whuppin," the crowd begin to mock. Black-Eyed Susan headed up the steps looking like a horse that had lost the race. Everyone stood around trying to hear Black-Eyed Susan's explanation. Miss Azalea was too tired to talk. She got the strap with the enlarged holes and beat Black-Eyed Susan on her back and rear end.

"It hurts me so much to whup you Black-Eyed Susan. Do you know how hard I'm working to try to take care of you. You don't know how much I have worked today. It makes me sick to come home and find out you have not done what I told you to do. Now, tomorrow you are gonna take all those clothes down, and wash them and hang them out again. If I come home, and you try to tell me some cockeyed story, I am going to use this strap on your naked behind," she promised.

Black-Eyed Susan got the lesson that time. At least she never tried to lie about the rain in the middle of a dry spell again.

Mrs. Azalea Samuels St. John was concerned about others. She knew from the deaths of her parents, grandparents, and two husbands how unexpected death or illness could bring tragedy to a family's door. These experiences had taught her the necessity of families sticking together and the importance of having a close churchgoing family. She raised her children to have these values, including Black-Eyed Susan.

Miss Azalea helped people when she saw they needed it. She didn't visit or spend time talking to neighbors. If someone died in the neighborhood, she would collect money from neighbors to buy flowers. She would call her friend, the Black lady who was a florist, and make sure to get a nice arrangement for the money she had collected. She would go to the funeral and see how the floral arrangement looked. She signed the sympathy card "Neighbors of Mulberry Lane."

If someone was laid off or fired, Miss Azalea would collect boxes of food and clothing to give to the family in distress. She never talked about what she did—she just gave in the best way she could.

As time passed, Miss Azalea found herself in the house alone. Black-Eyed Susan was the last one to leave. Unlike some women who experience the empty-nest syndrome, Miss Azalea lit up like a sunflower and kept sparkling. She had plenty of church work, several social clubs, in addition to her management of the Mulberry Lane Neighbors Club.

A gentleman, Mr. Leonard, who was a widower, was seen leaving Miss Azalea's home one morning. The neighbors gossiped, "Did you see Mr. Leonard's car was parked all night in front of Miss Azalea's last night?" One woman asked, "Wonder what they doin' in there all night?"

People gossiped but did not dare ask Miss Azalea or Mr. Leonard. Over time they developed a loving senior relationship. They were happy. They did things together, like go to senior parties, take short trips, or go to the grocery store together. It looked like Miss Azalea's years of hard work were over. She was enjoying the ease of life.

Miss Azalea did not discuss her life with people in the community. When someone tried to ask her a question, she considered too personal, she simply ignored the question or comment. She did not say a word. All the girls watched her. "When I grow up I want to be just like Miss Azalea," one little girl used to declare. "Why?," her mother asked. "Because, she has worked hard to raise a family, and now she has a love life all over again," girl told her mother.

Miss Azalea did not discuss her romance. The neighbors just got used to Mr. Leonard, a retired railroad worker, with what was rumored a good pension, coming to visit her at night. Mr. Leonard stayed some nights. Some nights he went back home. The senior-citizen couple became bolder with time. They started going everywhere together.

Some neighbors continued to whisper among themselves. Most people did not pay attention. They accepted Mr. Leonard like a new neighbor.

Miss Azalea died in her bathtub one night. Folks said she was "Gittin' ready for Mr. Leonard to come over. She had a Victoria Secret negligee laid out on the bed. Mr. Leonard went in there with his key and found her dead. They say she had a pretty smile on her face when she died." Some people wondered, "What was she thinking about?"

Miss Azalea set a good example for everyone who knew her. She was a supportive neighbor. She knew how to help without getting involved. She had knowledge of her community and compassion for people. Those who knew her as a human bouquet will always remember the love Mrs. Azalea Samuels St. John spread around Mulberry Lane.

7

Rock-Solid Resolve

Miss Clover was my Grandmother Hathor's friend. We lived across the street directly in front of them. Miss Clover lived with her daughter and son-in-law.

The Wall of Miss Clover's house began to crack from neglect.

The first time I asked my grandmother if I could visit Miss Clover, she unexpectedly said yes.

I hurried across the street before my grandmother changed her mind. She often cautioned me about visiting too often. "Don't wear out your welcome," she warned.

On my way up the steps, the military precision with which the bricks were laid caught my attention. I was excited. I wanted to ring the loud doorbell, which we could hear at our house, because Miss Clover was hard of hearing. She wore a hearing aid in her ear, which had a large battery that she wore inside her left breast right over her heart.

My visit was short and sweet. We sat on the porch. The concrete gray banister framing the porch was wide enough to sit or lay comfortably. In the summer, the red-and-white stripe awning shading the porch was a psychological defense against Mississippi's inescapable heat.

I rang the doorbell and waited impatiently for Miss Clover to come to the door. I rang the doorbell again, harder and longer. Finally, Miss Clover came to the door.

Miss Clover lived with her daughter and son-in-law, on one side of the four-room duplex, in the all-Black neighborhood on the east side of Meridian, Mississippi. Mrs. Clover Youngblood was a widow. But everyone called her Miss Clover.

Miss Clover's daughter, Eastermay Youngblood Stone, was just like her name—loud, hot, tough, and sassy. Her husband Edward Earl Stone was just the opposite. He was quiet, calm, introspective, and consistent.

Eastermay was a small woman, about 5-feet-2-or-3-inch tall, and weighed maybe 120 pounds. She could curse, and fight like a 200-pound man would. She specialized in the use of vulgarity as a defense mechanism. Even in ordinary conversations, she used obscenities routinely. She considered a greeting like, "Hey Mary. How you doin' you old ugly muthafucka," a friendly gesture. She did not mean a bit of harm. She just preferred to use profanity.

"That's the prettiest house on the block," neighbors conceded. It was constructed of attention-getting red bricks. Red Creeping Thyme flowerbeds were on both sides of the 15 steps leading up to the porch with the same flashing red bricks.

The cool-looking porch intrigued me. Miss Clover purchased the house after the death of her only son.

When Miss Clover opened the front door, she was happy to see me. I was about 12 years old—"Well hello little girl. How you doin'?"—she warmly asked.

"I am fine Miss Clover. My grandmother said I could come and sit with you a while," Topaz said.

I sat on the banister and looked up and down Mulberry Lane. None of the children were out playing.

We talked about what was going on in the neighborhood. I was anxious to share with Miss Clover a secret that I had not shared with anyone. "I got in trouble yesterday with my grandfather," I began. He told me to pick up some wood that scattered on the side of our house. I asked him, "why?" "He did not say a word; he started looking around the yard. I knew I was in trouble. I saw him headed toward the hatchet."

"Papa Lebni did not like to be questioned. I could see the anger in his face. I started running. By the time I reached the corner of the house, he had thrown the hatchet. It landed on the side of the house. It just missed my ankle. I went into the house with my grandmother to be safe."

I learned not to ever question my grandfather again.

Miss Clover turned and looked at me. "What you say honey," Miss Clover didn't have this old hearing aid turned on. I said, "'Oh,' its nothing Miss Clover."

That was the beginning of many afternoon visits with Miss Clover. I talked with her just like I thought a grown woman would. I was all of 12 maybe. I told her secrets about school, the boy I liked, my friends, and so on, with the understanding that she did not have the hearing aid turned on. I included stories about life in my home. I knew I wasn't supposed to talk about family business, but I had a lot of thoughts running around in my head. "What happens at home stays here," was one of my mother's first rules. I was relieved to get the things off my chest. Miss Clover seemed to be listening as she sipped a clear liquid in a juice glass she always had. Every once and a while she would say "Um, Uh." When I finished my confession, she would reach inside her bosom. "What you say honey?" Miss Clover didn't have this old hearing aid on. "Oh, nothing Miss Clove. I was just talking," I breathed. I told Miss Clover all my buried ideas when I had a chance to visit, because I knew my secrets were safe with the deaf woman.

Miss Clover and my grandmother, Hathor, were old women. They were of the same generation, but very different people. From a distance they looked alike. They wore A-lined dresses, usually with a small floral print, with short aprons, and colorful bonnets.

They were the elders of our community, born just before the 1900s. The only time you would see them together was when they took an occasional walk over to Price's store. As a child I took my place behind them watching and listening. "Hathor, you be our ears," Miss Clover would tease. "I'll be our eyes," she finished, without saying Mama Hathor was losing her sight. They were so respected, that old men gambling in a yard, would hide the dice when they saw them coming. All the men would tip their hats or bow their heads and mutter a greeting, "Afternoon ladies."

Some people poked fun at Miss Clover behind her back because she had a rare blood disease, which caused her to have warts all over her body, from the top of her head to the top of her feet. Some of the warts were a small as a pinhead; some were as large as a

When Mama Hathor and Miss Clover walked to Price's store, they were treated with respect by everyone.

golf ball. Sometimes the warts would change colors from blue/black to deep purple.

I felt special, like the protector, since my eyes and ears worked perfectly fine. At the store Mama Hathor bought Tub Rose Snuff, and Miss Clover bought Camel cigarettes without a filter.

Miss Clover passed the wart disease on to her daughter, Eastermay. This maybe one of things Eastermay was angry about in life. Also, the loss of her father and brother may have been a cause of her aggressive behavior. Still the disease did not stop Eastermay from living the kind of life she wanted. She was a party person. She knew how to make people laugh.

Sometimes, when she was taking care of her mother, and her mother's boyfriend, Buff, she would have a party for them in the middle of the day, in the middle of the week. Around mid-morning she would move the record player out on the porch. Then you would see her walk down to the bootleg whiskey house, about a half block down the street. Eastermay would come back with a brown paper sack. She would bring her mother,

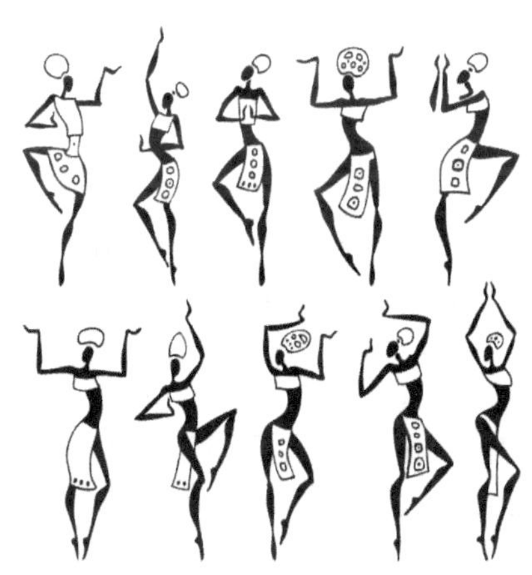

In spite of the oppression Black people always found a way to have a party.

Miss Clover, and Miss Clover's boyfriend, Buff, out onto the porch.

When Buff and Miss Clover were situated on the porch, Eastermay would give them a sip of the whiskey. Before long Miss Clover and Buff would be dancing on the front porch. Eastermay would put on some big band music, and those two old people would swing the day away.

When Eastermay was tired of the music the old people liked, she would put on some rhythm-and-blues tune that she liked. The scene instantly changed, because Eastermay was moved to dance. She would begin with a slow roll of her stomach muscles. By the time the rhythm reached her butt, some very graphic motion was occurring on Miss Clover's front porch.

"That's a shame, "Mama Hathor used to say. Mama Hathor did not drink whiskey. She did not like to be around people who were drinking. Miss Clover only came to visit Mama Hathor when she had not been drinking. Mama Hathor never went to Miss Clover's house.

The party would go on for hours, with Eastermay grinding and singing with the music. If somebody passed by on the street, and looked up at the strange sight, Eastermay would curse them out, "What you lokin' at mothafucka?"

When Eastermay felt it was time to prepare the evening meal, she would end the party. Everyone knew Eastermay was smart. But she never had a chance to use her mind. She got caught in the party life, and her frustration turned to anger. In spite of her vulgarity, everyone would acknowledge, "Eastermay is a good cook, and she keeps a clean house." Sometimes you could smell the pork chops she was frying floating in the neighborhood air.

"Alright, you old sons of bitches, it's time for me to fix my husband's supper." She would say this as matter-of-factly as the rising of the sun.

Buff, a tall, lean, handsome, brown-skinned man with graying hair, would speak up. "I am a veteran of the Spanish-American War. Don't nobody tell me when to stop dancing. Go do what you got to do, we ain't through just yet," he slurred. Wound up, he continued, "And hand me that bottle. I bought the whiskey."

"That's the only way you'd be up here you stupid mothafucks," Eastermay snapped back.

Eastermay would keep right on cursing. This time her wrath was directed toward Buff and the rest of the world. It didn't matter, she was mad. She would unplug the stereo and take what was left of the whiskey bottle into the house. The party was over.

The whole neighborhood could hear the abusive tone Eastermay used toward her husband Edward Earl. He walked up the hill from his job as a laborer for a local lumber company, whistling a blues tune knowing there would be a disturbance when he got home. Bobby Blue Bland was one of his favorite artists. He could whistle "Cry, Cry, Cry," "Farther On Up The Road," "I Stand Accused," as clear as a bell. I could feel the pain in the tone of his whistle, and by the songs he chose.

Edward Earl had what folks called a "good job." He was a big-boned red-skinned man with yellow undertones and light brown shadows. The neatly pressed blue work pants and shirt he wore to work every day bore the precision of Eastermay's skills at ironing. The black handle on his silver-colored lunch box was worn from many years of continuous use.

Whistling was Edward Earl's way of letting Eastermay know he was on his way. He had to give her some kind of warning, because there was no telling what she was doing. Eastermay could be throwing a party with a house full of men. From Monday to Thursday, Eastermay had a party with somebody in the middle of the day while Edward Earl was at work. She either had the party at her house or one of her friends. It was not above her to have a houseful of men once or twice a month at her house to party while Edward Earl was a work.

Folks often talked about the how crazy Edward Earl was for putting up with Eastermay. In that conversation they forgot Eastermay's skills. Beneath her harsh exterior Eastermay was an excellent housekeeper, cook, a laundress, bookkeeper, caretaker, and hostess. "You have to give a person their due," an old neighborhood woman would say. Edward Earl seemed to be following his own conscience. Or maybe Eastermay had some talent that the rest of the world was not privy to, except the other men she choose to spend time with.

On Fridays Edward Earl would whistle his way up the steps. "Here's the money," he would say emptying his pockets. "What took you so long mothafucka?"—Eastermay would snap as she counted the money. "Ah, Eastermay, don't start. Give me some cigarette money before you leave," he'd beg, looking down at his shoes. "I ain't giving you a damn thing," she swore switching down the steps. "Supper is on the stove," she hollered back over her shoulder. Most probably she would not be back until it was time to fix Edward Earl's breakfast and lunch on Monday morning. Some folks said she spent the weekend with several different men that she liked. Some said she spent the weekend at whiskey houses and clubs drinking up Edward Earl's money. Whatever she did, she was back home from Monday until Friday afternoon when Edward Early brought her his cashed paycheck.

Sometimes Eastermay would stay home on the weekend with Edward Earl. They would drink and play music on the porch. One night they were so drunk that they were lying on the porch floor. "We're gonna have a baby and name it Easterearl, if it's a girl, and Earleaster if it's a boy," Eastermay swore. That became a neighborhood joke. Edward Earl and Eastermay with a baby. God save the children.

One Friday afternoon Eastermay and Edward Earl were fighting. He was a big man, and she was a small woman. She ran down the steps out into the middle of the street. She pulled up her dress, dropped down her panties and patted her behind at Edward Earl. "Kiss my black ass, mothafucka, you and yo' dead mammy too." She shrieked. That is one of the worst things I have heard any human being say to another.

No matter how tough someone appears, there is always some weakness. Eastermay did not only raise hell with her family, if she were out in the street, she would pick fights with people twice her size. She was a fighting woman, full of anger. However, Eastermay was afraid of dogs. She would do all that cursing, fighting, insulting, yelling, but if a dog barked, she would take off running like a harmless cat. It was so funny to me see the neighborhood tough woman running up the hill from a harmless mutt.

One Easter my mother bought me a yellow ruffled dress trimmed in white lace. She also bought white patent leather shoes, with yellow socks trimmed in white lace. On Easter Sunday morning Grandmother Hathor got up early and helped me get dressed. My mother was not at home. I'm not sure where she was may be at work or housesitting for some White people she worked for.

Mama Hathor and I had managed to twist my short hair up with yellow and white ribbons. "You show do look pretty," Eastermay assured me. "Come walk with me around to Maw's house. I want to let her see how pretty you look."

Grandmother Hathor didn't say no; so I just took Eastermay by the hand and walked around the corner to Maw's, another neighborhood bootleg woman. Several men were sitting on the porch and inside the house. "The police is watchin' you," Maw said in a loud whisper to Eastermay. I know Eastermay said, "That's why I brought this child."

We were there for a few minutes while Maw poured some bootleg whiskey from a gallon jug into a half-pint bottle. When we got back to my house, my mother was waiting. It was about 10 minutes before 9 a.m. Mass starts at 9:30 a.m., at the Black Catholic Church I attended.

Eastermay told my mother. "She show looks pretty. I took her 'round to Maw's house, so they could see how cute she looks."

Eastermay left. "What are you doing going somewhere with Eastermay?"—my mother asked in a sharp tone. "I don't know," I sulked. "Go in there and take off those clothes. I am gonna spank your butt, so you will know to never go anywhere with Eastermay. Hurry up. Church starts in 30 minutes," she pointed the way with her left index finger." I went, undressed, and lay across the bed. My mother used her infamous left hand to spank me across my butt several times. "Not only don't you go nowhere with Eastermay, but you don't walk around showing off—you hear me?"—she kept tapping. No one else in the house, including Mama Hathor, said a word in my defense. Believe me, I never went anywhere with Eastermay again.

One fall, Mama Hathor and I were taking our afternoon nap. We heard the unusual sound of an ambulance. It stopped in front of Miss Clover's house. When they brought her out, her body was covered. "She's dead," a neighbor reported.

After the excitement of Miss Clover's passing, Mama Hathor I went to bed early, as usual. On this night, I slept with Mama Hathor.

We needed the comfort of each other's warm living body to reassure our sense of life. After we had been sleeping for several hours, some kind of animal woke us up scratching on the bottom of our screen door.

"Mama what's that?" I asked in a shaky little girl voice. "Nothin' be quiet," she replied. I peeped out the window. The Black raccoon, cat, opossum-looking creature went across the street, up the steps to Miss Clover's door. It scratched and made a weird noise. "Mama Hathor, listen," I insisted. We got up and watched the thing come back to our screen door. It assumed the same posture as before standing on its hind legs. It belted out the squealing sound again. "Oh, that's just Miss Clover telling us to watch out for the house," Mama Hathor concluded.

Eastermay lost the house soon after Miss Clover died. Eastermay and Edward Earl moved from the neighborhood.

For many years we heard no word of Eastermay. Every once in a while we would see Edward Earl in the Winn-Dixie grocery store. One time he told us Eastermay had had a stroke. "I had to put her in a nursing home," he said regretfully. Eastermay lingered in the nursing home for a decade.

Edward Earl went on with life as best he could. He kept his "good job" and made sure to take care of Eastermay's needs. He took up with another woman in time, but he never abandoned Eastermay. Sometimes he and his new girlfriend would go to the nursing home to visit Eastermay. Whether anyone else went, Edward Earl continued to pay for, work, and visit Eastermay. Whenever Edward Earl talked about Eastermay, you could see the love and pain in his eyes.

Eastermay got tired of suffering and died. Her cold Black body, in the nice casket, with the blue dress appeared to be in sharp contrast to the life she lived.

The soft blue dress she wore in death covered most of the warts, but you could see the one's on her face. Edward Earl sat in the front row of the funeral home service with his girlfriend and cried. His girlfriend put her arms around him and let him lay his head on her right shoulder as he mourned the death of his wife.

As we were leaving the service, one of Edward Earl's aunts told him, "Edward Earl, don't you feel bad. You walked all the way with this one. God will bless you," she ended.

Nature always offers a reprieve from harsh circumstances.

8

Chinaberry Playmates

By Furahaa Saba

Background of the story
Murders of Chaney, Goodman, and Schwerner

The **murders of Chaney, Goodman, and Schwerner**—also known as the **Freedom Summer murders**, the **Mississippi civil rights workers' murders**, or the **Mississippi Burning murders**—refers to events in which three activists were abducted and murdered in the city of Philadelphia, Mississippi, in June 1964 during the Civil Rights Movement. The victims were James Chaney from Meridian, Mississippi, and Andrew Goodman and Michael

The disappearance of the 3 Civil Right workers, Michael Schwerner, James Chaney, and Andrew Goodman, threatened to kill the summer joy of 1964 in Meridian, Mississippi.

Schwerner from New York City. All three were associated with the Council of Federated Organizations (COFO) and its member organization, the Congress of Racial Equality (CORE). They had been working with the Freedom Summer campaign by attempting to register African Americans in Mississippi to vote. Since 1890 and through the turn of the century, Southern states had systematically disenfranchised most Black voters by discrimination in voter registration and voting.

The three men had traveled from Meridian to the community of Longdale to talk with congregation members at a Black church that had been burned; the church had been a center of community organization. The trio was arrested following a traffic stop for speeding outside Philadelphia, Mississippi, escorted to the local jail, and held for a number of hours.[1] As the three left town in their car, they were followed by law enforcement and others. Before leaving Neshoba County, their car was pulled over. The three were abducted, driven to another location, and shot dead at close range. The bodies of the three men were taken to an earthen dam where they were buried.[1]

On January 6, 2005, a Neshoba County grand jury indicted Edgar Ray Killen on three counts of murder. When the Mississippi Attorney General prosecuted the case, it was the first time the state had taken action against the perpetrators of the murders. Rita Bender, Michael Schwerner's widow, testified in the trial.[58] On June 21, 2005, a jury convicted Killen on three counts of manslaughter; he was described as the man who planned and directed the killing of the civil rights workers.[59] Killen, then 80 years old, was sentenced to three consecutive terms of 20 years in prison. His appeal, in which he claimed that no jury of his peers would have convicted him in 1964 based on the evidence presented, was rejected by the Supreme Court of Mississippi in 2007.[60]

From Wikipedia, the free encyclopedia

The Story

The Chinaberry tree offers shade form the harsh Mississippi heat.

The Chinaberry tree gracing the yard of Katrinet and Augustina Proper distinguished their yard from other play areas in this Mississippi Black neighborhood.

On rare occasions, Topaz's Grandmother, Hathor, would let her visit the Proper girls to play. Grandmother Hathor did not believe in allowing children to spend too much time at other people's houses. "You don't know what might be going on." The only reason she consented to an occasional visit at the Proper girl's home was because their grandmother, Mrs. Helena Proper, was a schoolteacher. It was presumed that nothing improper would be occurring at Proper house.

Mrs. Proper was a widow, who was raising her son's children, two girls and a boy. No mention was ever made of the children's mother. Mrs. Proper had converted the grocery store her husband left into a home for herself and the grandchildren. The remolded store was a cinderblock building that the family used their worldly imagination to transform into a modest home.

The shed that had once been a storage space for the corner gro-cery store was a playhouse for the girls and boys at separate times. It was 1960; girls and boys did not play in mixed company. If the girls were playing in the playhouse, their brother found someplace else to play with his friends. The brown and black siding that covered the exterior walls made the little building stand out in the impoverished neighborhood. In summer or winter, a gleaming tin roof absorbed the intense Mississippi heat or shuddering cold air.

Playing dolls, school, and creating plays in that shed helped the girls extend beyond their physical boundaries. It was a private world. It was a place where they shut out the realities of racial conflict and class and gender issues that oppressed the very air of Mississippi in the 1960s. In this shed, there was no discussion of adult points of view. The play shed was a place where the three girls nourished their imaginations.

Katrinet was the oldest of the Proper girls. She was the leader of the playgroup. Katrinet would dream up creative ventures for the playgroup. The two younger girls would do everything they could to see the ideal come into reality. Katrinet was a shapely fair-skinned girl with long sandy brown hair.

Katrinet, Augustina and their brother would visit their father in New York for a few weeks each summer. Topaz would be anxious for their return. She knew there would be new things to talk about and do. One summer the Propers went to a Ballet.

As soon as they had a chance to meet in the play shed, Katrinet suggested, "Let's make up a ballet." Katrinet and Augustina took turns explaining to Topaz what a ballet was. They talked and worked for several days to come up with a storyline that would incorporate the unfamiliar dance form into a ballet. None of them had ever had a ballet class.

Katrinet took it upon herself to be the teacher. Augustina and Topaz imitated what Katrinet said were ballet steps. The month of August was spent rehearsing and refining what would surely be considered unclassical, by reputable ballet experts like Mr. Author Mitchell of the Dance Theatre of Harlem.

The girls were particular about how they would look. They carefully searched for clothes they could use as costumes. They searched, cut, and sewed until they had some semblance of what they wanted. Once the cardboard backdrops were painted, they were ready for their opening performance of "Our Friend: The Chinaberry Tree."

Mrs. Proper was the only audience member. The three girls performed the complete ballet for her in the living room of the Proper home. Mrs. Proper watched with expert attention. She generously applauded their awkward yet original ballet.

Mrs. Proper was a high school English and French teacher. She transferred the French accent to everyday Mississippi dialect. People in the community laughed at the way she sounded. "Where in the world did she get that funny talk?"—folks would say with quizzical facial expressions. Under their breath someone would mumble with disdain, "Trying to talk like white folks." Mrs. Proper would be sitting at her own table and say to one of the children, "Páss the bread please," as if she were in a French restaurant. The flat French accent she used would be scorned in Paris or New Orleans. Why doesn't she just say, "Pass the bread please," like everybody else?

Katrinet and Augustina patterned themselves vocally after their grandmother. The whole Proper family indulged in what the local people described as "uppity ways." That is they were perceived as people who were trying to act White even though they were Black. When individuals were described in this manner, they were usually fair-skinned with a soft texture of hair. "All you have to do is look at the back of their neck and you will see the nappy hair they're trying to hide," people would commonly remark.

Community folks treated Mrs. Helena Proper with a "whatever you say attitude." Guitar Slim, a neighborhood character in his own right, was an exception to this code of behavior. Guitar Slim looked Mrs. Helena Proper straight in the eyes and told her, "You crazy lady."

Watching the exchange between Mrs. Helena Proper and Guitar Slim was as stimulating as any devised recreation. Guitar Slim was an undersized nutmeg-brown-skinned man. Just like many men in the neighborhood, he drank either whiskey or beer every day. Professional people would probably label him as alcoholic. He probably never thought of himself in those terms. He was just doing what he needed to do to survive in an oppressive environment.

Guitar Slim was an excellent yardman. Black and White cus-

Impression of Guitar Slim, a neighborhood character who made up songs to ease the overbearing pain.

tomers sought his services. He had oral contracts in both communities. Whichever legally and socially segregated community he was working in, he behaved in the same manner. He would talk about the owners—"I don't know why they got all these flowers around the grass. The grass is enough," he would complain in a loud drunken mumble.

Everyone knew when Guitar Slim was in the neighborhood. He would arrive in the heat of the day pushing a two-wheeled lawn mower. He always carried a guitar strapped across his back. He carried his harmonica in his shirt pocket right over his heart. Whenever Guitar Slim got tired, he would sit down and play a tune to calm his nerves. When he finished playing the first song, he would take a sip of whiskey from the bottle he carried in his left hip pocket. Guitar Slim had a reputation for doing outstanding work. Owners and neighbors just had to put up with the fact that he was going to talk loud, play and sing music, as well as drink some kind of alcohol.

Guitar Slim made up original folk songs to deal with life's conflicts. The verses he made up about Mrs. Helena Proper were startling. When he finished cutting the yard, Guitar Slim and Mrs. Helena Proper would have a disagreement over price and precision. Guitar Slim would really show his talent them. He would stand on the edge of the curb and start testifying with his guitar and harmonica about Mrs. Helena Proper. He played and sang loud enough for the neighborhood to hear his complaint. "Ain't nothin' like a cheap Black widow woman," he sang one day accompanying himself on the guitar. "She just as bad as a poor white woman," he played and sang. "They both want you to work, but they don't want to pay," he let his harmonica take over. "You ain't gonna work me to death Miss Lady, for a little bit of money," he belted above the guitar.

Guitar Slim was a street person. He did not care about Mrs. Proper's rules. He was concerned about the basics of food, clothing, shelter, a guitar string, and enough alcohol to have a fun outlook on the misery around his life.

"Oh that's too much," she would complain every time Guitar Slim asked for his $5.00 for cutting the yard. After their standoff, Mrs. Proper would give in, "Here Mr. Slim," she'd say handing him the rumpled money. She did not agree with the price or care for his refusal to go beyond the requirements of the job. "I'm not gonna pick up your trash. I'll mow around it. But you have to clean your own yard. That's not in the job. You know what day I'm coming over here. You ought to clean up before I get here," he would slur back at the expected request.

Mrs. Proper would stare baffled by the exchange. She would shift her weight from one side to the other. Her fair skin would turn redder. She would use the pencil she wore stuck in her dyed red hair to scratch her head to demonstrate her confusion. When she handed over her money, she was giving in to the fact that she would never understand Guitar Slim. She was not a Black Street expert. More importantly, she could not understand why Guitar Slim would not obey as the children in her classroom or home. Mrs. Helena Proper was unaccustomed to having her authority challenged. Pushing the round thick black eye glasses up on her small pointed nose, her body exuded a portrait of a schoolteacher confronting a behavioral pattern that was not described in the teacher's manual.

The girls would watch this exchange from underneath the Chinaberry tree that graced the shed. The Chinaberry tree gave a welcome breeze during the intensely hot summers. Usually, they would be playing inside the shed when they would hear the rising voices of Mrs. Proper and Guitar Slim. Knowing there was going to be a performance, the girls took their places underneath the Chinaberry tree.

While they were watching the exchange, they would collect chinaberries. This was another one of their creative summer projects. After they gathered the chinaberries, they would assemble them in groups of similar size. Like diligent jewelry makers they would string the berries together with a needle and white thread. "We can sell them," Katrinet convinced them. The young entrepreneurs got permission to peddle the natural jewelry to homes they were allowed to visit. They had very few sales, and lots of fun. They were not discouraged. They made the necklaces all summer. The ones they didn't sell, which were many, they used as costume accents in other performances of poetry and plays that they presented for Mrs. Proper.

If the girls managed to sell on China Berry necklace for one penny, it was like a million dollars to them. They would report the sale to Mrs. Proper, who would reward the girls with enough nickels and dimes to buy a treat from the snowball man.

Even though Topaz, Katrinet, and Augustina lived in the same neighborhood, their lives were worlds apart. The fact that Mrs. Proper was a schoolteacher, and the children's father an architect, broadened the world for them. The Proper children had spent their early childhood in New York. No one in Topaz's family had finished high school. Topaz knew they were people like everybody else, but she appreciated the fact they had innovative ideas.

Three seeds of artistic expression were planted under the Chinaberry tree. The three girls became lifelong practitioners and supporters of the arts.

I am so thankful for the love of art that was planted in my soul,
under the Chinaberry Tree.

9

Bright Blue House!

Miss Paradise Bosom Byrd owned the Bright Blue House. She gave the bewildered community of Negroes something to talk about every day of her life. Whether she was fencing her yard, putting on a new roof, touching up the infamous blue paint, or putting an alcoholic off her property, she added a flavorful zest to rumors passed on during soul food dinner and supper conversations. Miss Paradise's reputation was so notorious, that she often inspired sermons of ministers in the local Black and White churches.

Old timers continued to talk about her achievements years after her death. All the busybodies reporting about Miss Paradise ignored the fact that she owned her property in this modest Black neighborhood in Meridian, Mississippi. The people of this community, including Miss Paradise, were descendants of Africans, who had lived and survived the tragedy of slavery. Quick to deny their real ancestry, they often fell into the trap designated for them by White racist. "I ain't from no Africa." This same line of reasoning perpetuated the "crab in the barrel"

Whiskey, though illegal at the time, was used to bury the pain of living.

mentality. This is an attitudinal expression that pulls anyone down who tries to make it to the top. Victims of the racially organized oppression, they caught a glimpse of truth and hope during the Civil Rights Movement, which spoke to their deepest desires. Some people wanted to succeed.

Miss Paradise was a Black woman trying to take care of her family, without the benefit of education or opportunity. In fact, as a Black woman in America's South of the 1960s she carried the weight of the White man's oppression across the length of her spine. She was trying to get a piece of the American dream for herself and her family.

Mostly men and a few women frequented the Bright Blue House. The royal blue Sears and Roebuck paint saturating the wood-frame 1960s-style house lit up the Southern Black neighborhood like a flashing lighthouse. It was different from other houses in the neighborhood. Standing as alluring as the Statue of Liberty, the community landmark lured willing and unwilling customers like a passionate lover.

Any woman who went to Miss Paradise's house was considered low class. Everyone who left the shocking Bright Blue House was stepping higher when they left than they were when they came. Some would wander out in a stupor.

Miss Paradise Bosom Byrd was a bootlegger. There were other bootleggers in the community, but Miss Paradise, as she was called, was the queen of bootlegging. She appeared to have more customers, more connections to get the illegal whiskey she sold, and more money. Miss Paradise was a replica of the original Aunt Jemima. She was a huge Black woman with kind, dark brown eyes, and she wore a head scarf covering her head. Her inviting smile and friendly ways comforted many people.

Miss Paradise lived in the house with her grown daughter Lope. Lope was a lanky 6-foot tall cherry-black woman. Lope had a baby girl everyone called Peanut. Junior, the teen age son, of Miss Paradise's oldest daughter, who was in prison for murdering a man, was the only male living in the house.

No one remembered how Miss Paradise came into ownership of this property. Her husband had been dead for so long people didn't talk about him anymore. That was quite an accomplishment, because the people of this community thrived on gossip. What else was there to do?

Miss Paradise sold bootleg whiskey to take care of her family and property. The clear locally brewed moonshine liquor was commonly called, "Poot Whiskey." Poot whiskey is a powerful potion. "It will make you holler at the moon," experts declare.

Miss Paradise was risking her life by selling illegal alcohol. The American South at that time was a hot bed of racial violence. Segregation laws separating the Blacks from the White population were strictly enforced. In order for Miss Paradise to get the "poot whiskey," a White man had to come to her house. She did not have a whiskey still in her backyard. Folks talked about her just because a White man went to her house. "Somethin' ain't right," neighborhood critics muttered.

Meridian, like many Southern small towns of the 1960s was characterized by a close-knit community in a predominantly rural and agricultural setting. The town had a main street, where local businesses and shops were clustered. Social life revolved around community events, churches, and schools. During this period, Mississippi, like much of the Southern United States, experienced the challenges of racial segregation and civil rights struggles. The town reflected the social dynamics of the time, with separate facilities for Black and White residents.

Blue Laws were enforced. These laws made it illegal to sell or consume alcohol. They were laws left on the books from the days of Prohibition. A strong Bible Belt Christian community reinforced them. These laws did not stop the sale of "poot whiskey." Miss Paradise had plenty of business.

"She must be in cahoots with the police," folks said, who turned their nose up at Miss Paradise. "They say she pays them," another offered. The police came to Miss Paradise's house several times to raid. She had already announced to her customers that they would be coming. No customers went to her house on the day of the planned raid.

"Police comin' to Paradise's house tomorrow," folks would be saying. "Guess I'm gonna go to Buddy's to get my drank tomorrow," serious drinkers decided. Buddy was a bootlegger who lived out in the country.

When the police car arrived, Miss Paradise would be sitting on the front porch with Lope, Peanut, and Junior. She kept lush green plants surrounding much of the porch. She sat right in front of the screen door, the only place that could be seen from the street. As the police opened the gate of the Sears & Roebuck fenced yard to walk up to the red-brick walkway, Miss Paradise greeted them. "How ya'll doin' Mr. Jed. Come on in," she said inviting them from the neat yard onto the porch.

"Fine Auntie, How you," the red neck officer spoke.

"Oh, I'm tolerably well, for an old woman, Suh," Miss Paradise chatted.

"We can't complain, Auntie," Mr. Jed began as he spat tobacco out the side of his mouth. He showed her a piece of paper.

"What's that Mr. Jed," the matriarch asked.

"Somebody called and said you sellin' poot whiskey out here," the policeman reported.

"Oh, Mr. Jed, you know that ain't true. I'm just a po' widow woman. I ain't got no money to buy no whisky. All I got is what the welfare gives me, and my commodity," she replied. Commodity was a program that distributed food to poor people, like milk, eggs, and cheese.

"You see I got my daughter and two grand chillum here. It takes every penny I get to feed and clothe them and keep a roof over our heads. I don't know why folks be callin' you and lyin' on me?" she questioned.

"Well Auntie, "I'm satisfied that you ain't out here breakin' the law. You know you can go to jail for sellin whiskey. Ain't yo' daughter up there in the state prison," the officer picked.

"Yassaw, and it's a terrible place. You know I ain't tryin' to go to no penitentiary. I got my family whats here to take care of," Miss Paradise reiterated.

"All right Auntie," Officer Jeb said. "Just so we understand one another." He turned and headed back to his patrol car.

Miss Paradise got up and went back into the house. The next morning, she started selling whiskey as soon as the sun came up.

"What you want a single or a double," she asked the first customer.

"Double," it's been along time," he said.

"Just day befo' yesterday," she shot back.

"Here's yo' money woman. That's all you think about," the old man complained.

"Just so you give me all my money on the first," she reminded him.

Miss Paradise was a businesswoman. She ran a credit business for men who received welfare or social security checks. She would give them credit throughout the month. When their checks came, they would bring them to her. She would cash the checks, charge them a fee for cashing the check, and take her money for the whiskey they got on credit. She kept good books and made the men sign for any whiskey they got, even if they signed with a x because they could not read.

Junior, her grandson, suffered the most devastating effect of this lifestyle. He became a teenage alcoholic. All the men he saw round him were serious drinkers. He tried to do what they did. His young body could not handle the harsh chemical invasion. He started stumbling up the street, talking out of his head like many of the men who left Miss Paradise's house. He stopped school when he was about 14 to live this alcoholic life.

Lope, Miss Paradise's tall, strong daughter, would be standing around the house to bounce anybody up against the wall or onto the street if they tried to cause a disturbance.

Miss Paradise ran a "respectable" house. Even though a lot of men came, she did not allow them to linger. "You ain't gonna sit here. I got grandchildren," she informed anyone who tried to stay longer than she allowed. The rule was to stay long enough to down a shot or two, pay, or sign for the whiskey and leave. If they bought a half-pint bottle, Miss Paradise had a place in the back yard where they could sit and play dominoes, cards, or shoot dice while sipping the strong "Poot Whiskey." A limited number of men, depending on how she felt that day, could sit around as long as someone was buying a bottle. No shots were sold in the yard.

An impression of Miss Paradise watchin over her flock.

A lot of men and a few women get very drunk over time drinking Miss Paradise's "poot" whiskey. Except for the whiskey sale, the house seemed normal, clean, and well kept.

"Did you hear 'bout Miss Paradise?" a gossiping old man asked the Christian women's circle sitting out under the trees in the neighborhood park.

"Naw," they murmured in unison, anticipating the details. "Well she didn't know the police was comin' this time," the old man stated—"she was sittin' at the kitchen table eatin' a piece of chocolate cake. Ya'll know Paradise make a mean chocolate cake. The Sheriff kicked the front door in. Paradise got up and went to the back room and got the gallon of "poot whiskey" she keeps back there while they were in the living room explaining to Lope about the warrant. Paradise sat the jog down in the toilet and sat on top of it. When the police opened the bathroom door all he saw was big fat Black Paradise sitting on the commode," the man gossiped grinning.

"Oh, I'm sorry, Auntie, "old man Jeb claimed.

"You ought to be," she told him. "A woman can't even use the bathroom without ya'll botherin' her," Paradise mumbled.

The storytelling man cackled, loving the attention he was getting from all the so-called Christian women in the park. "They left," he continued, "Neva did find no whiskey."

"They gonna catch her someday," one woman concluded, "God don't like ugly.

"They say she sleeps with the sheriff," another woman chimed in.

The gossiping man left the women satisfied for the hours of talk about Miss Paradise. True or not, the talk was always entertaining and took their minds off their own problems. Miss Paradise was not welcome in their circle.

Miss Paradise continued her business until she got too old, sick, and tired. The years of evading the law, and dealing with alcoholics, and their debt took their toll. She lived long enough to pass on a house to her grandchildren. Miss Paradise passed away. Her work on earth was completed.

Lope didn't like life too much after her mother died. Soon afterward she succumbed and went to be with her mother. This left Peanut and Junior in the house. Peanut went to school and became a nurse. She tried to help Junior, but crack, a free base form of the stimulant cocaine that can be smoked, took over his life. "You got to go," she told him, the last time he stole something from the house while she was at work.

Peanut had a daughter and continued to maintain her grandmother's property.

She eventually bought the eyesore house next door, tore it down, and constructed a lovely sculpture garden in its place.

Time continued to pass. Peanut raised her daughter, and helped her raise her children. "I still miss Big Mama," she'll tell you any day.

Peanut replaced the faded blue paint with a decent-home-looking gray. The veins of Miss Paradise Bosom Byrd still fly around the family home, hovering like protective wings over the lives of her descendants.

10

Fundamental Terror

Living in the valley in the middle of a sharp curve in the Southern Black neighborhood has its advantages and disadvantages. Meridian, Mississippi was caught in the middle of the Civil Rights Movement of the 1960s. The people, Black and White, had no choice. "Outsiders" in the minds of both races had invaded their Southern cultural traditions. War was imminent. There were only two sides—Black and White. The warriors of this modern American insurrection were not concerned about the remaining races of the world. The air was filled with the taste of blood mixed with the commitment to love God, family, and community.

Sounds of children's laughter and squabbles rang through the air of the vacant lot on the west side of Mr. Joshua and Honey Soul's home. The joyful noise chased away fears of the conflict between the races instilled in the merchant town. There were eight children— four girls and four boys. Mr. and Mrs. Soul were a young couple who loved having a big family. Both of them played with and indulged each one of their children. They loved baseball. It was a daily ritual for the whole family to play some kind of ball before supper. They played football, basketball, and baseball according to the season. Of course, other children came and joined in. Everyone was welcome.

On the other side of the vacant lot sitting on a slab of raised concrete was the cinderblock store constructed and owned by Mr. John

Playing baseball was one way to relieve stress.

Solomon. His wife, whom everyone called Miss Doll Baby, was the only child of her mother who folks said had "a little money put away." Miss Doll Baby managed the store. She sold milk, eggs, a few canned goods, and a limited variation of meats. Candy, chewing gum, and dill pickles for children were the bread and butter of the John and Doll Baby Solomon's "Mom & Pop Corner Operation." In the back of the store Mr. Solomon added an apartment when he was building the store. Miss Doll Baby's mother, the oldest women in the community, lived within walking distance of the store. It was maybe 20 steps. The Solomon family had four children—two girls and two boys. The Solomon's spent most of their days at the store, but they lived several blocks away in a home Mr. Solomon had built himself.

These two families shared the neighborhood of pine top trees, wild turkey, chickens, and squirrels running loose. They shared the air and the vacant lot with the depressed red dirt clearing. Luscious bushes and trees surrounded the naturally formed playground. The abundantly rich environment was referred to as "The Valley." Even though the two families shared Mother Earth's bounty, they maintained contrasting lifestyles.

Picture of two black boys playing.
One mistake can change your life forever.

The Soul and Solomon families operated on the principle of patri-archy. The contrasting characters of the fathers set a greater part of the mood, activities, and standard of living. Meridian, like many African American communities, was a victim of the "strong Black woman" syndrome. This was a line of reasoning that catered to the fact that there are so many households headed by females, that most wom-en didn't have any choice but to wear the pants as well as dresses in their families. This is a leftover defense from the days of slavery, when Black women were often forced to negotiate issues for the family with the White power structure, because Black men were so feared. Black men posed the greatest threat because of their potential to produce offspring. In modern times, this conviction was transferred into an accusation that Black women could get in doors closed to Black men. This type of irrational thinking caused a deep-seated division in the relationship between Black men and women. It was the old rule of divide and conquer. This unwritten creed clouded relationships be-tween Black women and men propagating an undercurrent of suspi-cion, jealousy, and exploitation. During this time period, most Black communities described themselves as "Matriarchal."

This was not the case in the families of Mr. Joshua Soul and Mr. John Solomon. They were the primary breadwinners in their families. Mr. Soul owned a landscaping business, with contracts from the city and state. Mr. Solomon owned a bricklaying business. His reputation and skill were so well known that he could pick and choose the jobs he wanted.

It was more than a notion for a Black man to own a successful business in the Civil Rights climate of the 1960s Southern America. Black people still did not have the right to vote. In fact, the people of Meridian were on edge in the summer of 1964 because three Civil Rights Workers had been murdered in Philadelphia, Mississippi, which was about 40 miles.

The three Civil Rights workers—Andrew Schriener, Mark Goodman, and James Chaney—ran an office for SNCC (Student Nonviolent Coordinating Committee) in Meridian. In order to teach people how to pass the voting test, they had to teach many people how to read. During the summer of 1964 they ran the "Freedom School." This was a school that was set up in what had once been The Baptist Seminary, for training Black ministers. The Seminary had closed, but the two-story building was an ideal place to run the Freedom School. White volunteers from northern schools and cities came to teach basic reading, writing, math, Mississippi History, as well as politics. Children and adults attended the various classes. The Soul and Solomon children attended some classes at the Freedom School.

The Mississippi establishment did not sit by quietly as the Civil Rights activities were being organized. They pressured people in the press. The police harassed people. In addition to the strong arm of the state, there was also increased activity of the Ku Klux Klan. The Klan would put on their white sheets and have a parade in downtown Meridian.

These historical realities did not escape the people in Meridian. Mr. Joshua Soul and Mr. John Solomon knew what a risky job it was to protect their families. On a daily basis they encountered White men and women who had only been trained for generations to treat Black people as slaves or slave workers. Both men knew the torture of being in the presence of White people who would only call them boy. "'Boy,' I want this grass to look like Jesus could walk on it. You hear me?" "Boy, lay them bricks over there"; these are but some examples of dehumanizing attempts both men endured on a daily basis. While each man designed his own approach to the process, they had similar yet different styles of achieving their goals.

Mr. Soul and Mr. Solomon were intelligent Black men. Whatever they were called, regardless of the negative attitudes they endured, they knew how to initiate, get, and maintain a contract. They did what was necessary to raise their families.

While there was a strong male dominance in the valley of Meridian, there was also a passionate feminine efflorescence. Mrs. Honey Soul was an energetic, fun-loving mother. Having given birth to eight children at home with only the help of her husband, she was a shapely, bronze-colored, outgoing mom. Children from all over Meridian loved Mama Honey. Honey Soul welcomed the children with open arms, a big smile, and a hug. She invited children into her home and watched them as they played in the valley.

In addition to being an indulgent mom, Honey Soul was a romantic. She would wait outside for Joshua to come home. She would hug and kiss him like a newlywed every evening. Although Honey Soul was playful, she was a hardworking smart woman. She attended the local public school where she graduated. She kept the books for her husband's business and for the household. She cooked three meals a day for her eight children. When school was in session, she made eight fresh lunches every morning, before breakfast. Honey Soul often played in the Valley with her children. Even if she was not playing, she kept a watchful eye. She knew just when to intervene to stop a dis-

Mrs. Honey Soul enjoyed her family as well as having a party.

agreement among children. You could see love in all of Honey Soul's actions toward children.

Just like a rose bush, Honey Soul had thorns in her side. Honey Soul was concerned with the happiness of her children. No matter what everyone else did, she followed her own brand of child-raising. You had the sense that Honey Soul treated her children like she wanted to be treated. She did the best she could to keep a decent roof over their heads, made sure they had plenty of good food, bought them the latest fashions, and made sure they had quality play equipment. On the other hand, she used ideas grounded in the Holiness Church she grew up in, as the foundation on which she was standing. On Sunday morning, Honey Soul got up and made sure all eight of her children were dressed and had breakfast before they walked the several blocks to Family Circle Holiness Church. After Sunday school, the children would stay for 11:00 a.m. church service. The Soul children would be at church until at least 3:00 p.m. Pastor Huldah Aaron, one of the few women ministers in the area, was longwinded. Dressed in her flowing white gown she would preach and dance to the bass guitar and drums behind her until she had the whole church riled up and shouting.

The Bible say, "…suffer little children to come unto me and forbid them not, for of such is the kingdom of God," Honey told a friend. "I'm glad to send them, because" she smiled coyly, "It's the only private time I have with Joshua. You know me and Joshua, we got to have time together."

Miss Doll Baby was just the opposite of Honey. She was a heavyset, fair-skinned woman with big welcoming breasts. Miss Doll Baby graduated from a local Black Catholic school. In addition to English, mathematics, and history, Miss Doll Baby had studied Latin and classical music. She spent so much time at the store that she had Mr. Solomon move the upright family piano into the store. Since the store wasn't extremely busy, Miss Doll Baby had plenty of time to practice the Italian arias she loved. While most people in the surrounding area were playing rhythm and blues on their radios or stereos, Miss Doll Baby would be practicing a classical number. Her clear, high-pitched soprano voice floated through the bottom like a singing bird. Her musical journey occurred in between efforts to school her children in the store during the summer months and taking care of her mother.

Whereas the Soul children were outside playing baseball, the Solomon children were inside the store neatly dressed reading or working on math problems. Sometime late in the afternoon Miss Doll Baby would let them venture over to the valley to play for a short time before supper.

A resemblance of Miss Doll Baby as a Young Woman.

One day the Soul and Solomon children were playing in the valley's luscious open space. The older boys were playing touch football. The girls were taking turns on the swing in the front yard of the Soul home. The two youngest boys, Quincy Soul and Joseph Solomon, both 5 years old, took a while deciding what to play.

"Let's play some catch," Quincy suggested.

"Nah, I'm not good at catching a ball," Joseph confessed.

"OK. We can find something else," Quincy quickly agreed. "What do you like?"

"I like chess, which I'm sure you don't like," Joseph admitted.

"It's not that I don't like it," Quincy explained, "I just don't know how to play. Maybe you can teach me," he said hoping to find a friend outside his family who was his own age. "Can you get your chess set? We only have checkers and monopoly."

"If I go inside, my mom won't let me come out again," Joseph disclosed.

"Forget it," Quincy mildly suggested. Let's play Cowboys and Indians. We got two guns and two holsters for Christmas," the child said regaining his sense of hope. "I know where they are, my mom won't mind if we play with them," Quincy said, leading his friend toward the Soul home.

Miss Honey saw the two youngsters coming toward the house. "What you all looking for Quincy?"—she asked as the boys reached the front door. "We want to play Cowboys and Indians. Isn't that great Mama? I have my own friend to play with." "Yes, it is Quincy. A good friend is a precious thing," she said sweating over a pile of shirts she had to finish ironing.

Quincy went in the house and found two holsters, one gun among the pile of toys scattered about the den. "Mom, I can't find the new gun", he yelled. "Look in the living room Quincy, I can't keep up with every single thing." Quincy searched the house. He was getting frustrated, because he knew Joseph didn't have long to play before his mom would be calling him inside. "'Oh', here's a little gun," he said, fumbling behind the makeshift bar that Miss Honey sometimes used when she was having a poker party. "I'll take that one, and give Joseph the big gun," he resolved. Joseph was anxiously waiting outside. He saw the big children enjoying their playtime. He hoped Quincy would hurry up, so he could have a little time to play. "Mother will be calling me soon," the tiny bookworm thought pushing his glasses up on his face. "I found them, Joseph," Quincy finally appeared. "I couldn't find the gun for this holster. So, I'll give you the big gun. You play the Indian. I'll use this little gun and be the Cowboy. There's a place on the edge of the valley, where there are lots of trees. We can have our own war, and no one can find us." Quincy said excitedly, leading the way.

The boys headed for the secret war ground. As they were working out the rules of their war game, Quincy took his gun out of the holster, and pointed it just above Joseph's glasses, in the middle of his forehead. "See I'll go POW," he was explaining. The 22-caliber single gunshot echo punctured the childish wonder of the valley.

Joseph's blood was gushing from his head. He was thinking about the pain but couldn't talk. Quincy was running from their hiding place screaming, "He's bleeding, he's bleeding." By the time everyone assembled around the spot, blood and panic was running rampant.

Mr. Solomon happened to be in the store. He came over and saw his son lying in the bush with blood gushing from his forehead. Being a quick-minded man, he picked the child up and headed for his truck. "We got to get to the hospital," he kept repeating. While carrying Joseph to the truck, he also had to calm his wife. Miss Doll Baby started screaming as soon as she saw her husband and son. "Calm down Doll Baby," John Solomon directed his wife. "Get the other children and bring them inside." John Solomon was rushing with his son's life in his hands.

Miss Honey was talking to Quincy, trying to find out what happened. "I thought it was a toy," the child kept muttering. "Come on, baby let's go call daddy." Onlookers stood around in horror trying to make sense of the instant tragedy. The police came and tried to get a report of what happened. By the time Mr. Soul got home, Mr. Solomon was returning from the hospital. "Joseph is dead," he said, more to himself than to the lingering shocked crowd.

The death was ruled an accidental homicide. One moment in time changed the entire tone of the valley. From that day forward the Solomon children stayed on their side of the valley. The Soul Children stayed in their yard. What was once a naturally landscaped playground became an overgrown dumping ground.

Miss Doll Baby never recovered from the death of her baby child. She stopped singing pretty classical songs and started singing mourning songs. She stopped teaching the children at the store. Instead, she left them at home while she ran the store. Her sorrow planted the seed for breast cancer. She suffered through the loss of both of her breasts. She died a few years after Joseph.

Mr. Solomon held Miss Doll Baby's wake at the family home. He had the casket rolled into the living room. Miss Doll Baby was laid up in the casket in an ivory lace dress. A matching lace veil was draped over the casket opening. Viewers could see but not touch Miss Doll Baby. The three remaining Solomon children sat in order just as their mother had taught them. A Catholic Priest said a short prayer, and the casket was closed. People stood around consoling the family as a version of the Requiem Mass played in the background.

Honey Soul was distraught about the accident also. She started seeing a "two headed doctor." This is a preacher-man type who can fix things for the right amount of money. "I want to have the spell moved from Quincy," she told the crooked man. "Ever since that accident he ain't been right," she told the two-headed doctor. "I have to do a lot to get rid of that cloud," the sly man told Honey. "I have to go to the woods and get some special leaves for you to rub on him. It will take maybe a year for the magic to work. It's gonna cost a lot." "I don't care how much it cost," Honey promised. "I take care of Joshua's books, I'll get the money," the distraught woman decided. The two-headed doctor started coming to the Soul home on a weekly basis. "She gives him money in a brown paper sack," the neighbors gossiped.

One day Mr. Soul went to the bank, he wanted to withdraw $70,000 to buy a new truck. "I want to pay in cash," he told the banker. The banker was left to explain to Mr. Joshua Soul, "I'm sorry Joshua, there is no money in this account. There is exactly five dollars, just enough to keep it open." "But I been giving my wife money to put in there. I know it should be at least $100,000." "I'm sorry Joshua, but here is the record of withdrawals signed by your wife," the banker showed Mr. Soul the signatures which he knew were authentic, but unbelievable, nonetheless.

Joshua Soul was a happy-go-lucky man. He had a big easy smile and a positive outlook on life. "Honey must have put that money in a different account," he told himself on the short drive home. He parked the truck in the curve in front of his house. He would only be here a minute. Just long enough to find out which bank account Honey had put his money into. He had made up his mind to buy the new truck today. He had more state contracts and needed an additional truck to keep up with the demand of landscaping state-owned property. "Honey, I just went to the bank, they say it's no money in that savings account. You know, the one I opened just to save for the truck," he began casually. "I been meaning to tell you Joshua," she started. "You know those treatments I get for Quincy, well they been costing more than I thought they would. It got to where I couldn't pay the doctor out of the household money. So, I kept going to the bank to get his money. He'd been doing so well with Quincy," Mrs. Honey Soul replied in a trembling voice. "You mean he cost almost $100,000," the usually calm man squeaked. "What's a hundred thousand dollars for the happiness of our baby boy?"—she screamed back. "You can make some more money. But he only has one life. I'm determined he's going to be somebody. Why should he be punished with that old nasty spell, when money can buy his way out? You know I told you from the beginning, I want the best for my children," Honey Soul argued.

Joshua Soul knew there was no use in debating with his wife. "All right Honey let's not fight. I'm going to go back to the bank and get a loan. I'll have to get extra more contracts to pay the loan off. I don't like owing these white people too long. They always try to take something back from a Black man. We have to be serious about saving this time. Is there enough money in one of the other accounts to get $10,000 for a down payment?"—he asked trying to keep his mind on his goal for the day. "Um, um," Miss Honey shook her head. "Give me the number," Mr. Soul requested. Miss Honey went to the safe where she kept important papers. She had dreaded this day for so long; silent tears ran down her face. She knew the disappointment her husband and lover felt. Yet, she had to hold on to the hope for her son. "I don't know what to do about Quincy, but I know this can't continue. We are going to start again today," the distraught father figured.

Joshua Soul drove back to the bank. The banks were not accustomed to making large loans to Black men. Joshua Soul had established good credit. After all, the bank would own the truck. "If I get behind in these payments, they are going to take this truck right away," he thought leaving the bank with the approved loan. There was no doubt that the bank would take the truck if they got the slightest chance. He made up his mind that he would have to work much harder than he was already working to protect his investment. "What am I going to do about Honey and the two-headed doctor?" crept into his thoughts processes, as he searched for the strength to keep on. He pushed the fact that he didn't know to the back of his mind. He got up everyday, went to work, came home, and played with his children, and tried not to be mad at Honey.

The two-headed doctor continued to come to the Soul home. Quincy was improving. He had a natural flair for baseball. The two-headed doctor claimed credit for his desire to play again. People in the neighborhood knew that the boy had inherited his father's athletic ability. Joshua Soul had turned down a chance to pitch with the Negro Baseball league because he had a family to take care of. Instead, he spent many evenings teaching his boys the tricks of the trade.

One evening Mr. Joshua Soul came home from laying grass at the county hospital. He backed his new truck into the yard. He did not see Precious, his youngest daughter, as she ran behind the truck to greet him. Precious screamed as the rear right wheel crushed her skull. Mr. Soul jumped out of the truck. He picked his bleeding daughter up in his arms, her brains, oozing onto his work clothes and all the cab of the truck, as he and Honey tried to rush her to the hospital. Precious died in Honey's arms before they made it to the hospital.

A dark cloud hung over the valley. The happy ring of children playing was forever gone. Honey kept giving money to the two-headed doctor, to try to correct things. Joshua was finally forced to face the fact that he could not trust his wife. He hired a bookkeeper. That was the beginning of the divorce. Honey took to selling liquor out of the living room to pay the two-headed doctor. Joshua did not know what to do to help his high school sweetheart. Finally, he just moved out. After the divorce decree, Honey mourned herself into the ground before she was 40.

Joshua married a much younger woman. He started all over again and had four daughters with his new wife. Quincy was drafted to pitch for the Atlanta Braves. He played a few years before an injury forced an early retirement.

Each family wore the veil of sorrow caused by the deaths of children and their mothers. All of the other children survived the tragedies. The Soul children kept up the Holiness tradition established by their mother. The Solomon children practiced Catholicism as their mother had taught them. Eventually all of the children married and moved away to raise their own families in better conditions. Both families grew and prospered, but they could not escape the fundamental cloud of terror they had lived in Meridian, Mississippi.

All the children learned that even though there are sometimes dark clouds, life is also filled with sunshine.

11

Crawling to Safety

By Furahaa Saba

Topaz was exposed to business ownership from Black people in Meridian. Segregation Laws prohibited the mixing of races. Black people had their own section of town with a hotel, several restaurants, a doctor's office, a pharmacy, a beauty school, and several beauty shops and barber shops. There were many seamstresses in town who could make your clothes for you if you didn't want to go through the humiliation of buying from White storeowners whose stores were located on the main street.

Image of downtown Meridian, Mississippi.

Mrs. Cloverine Summer crawled with her mother, father, sister, and brother from Marian, Mississippi, about 10 miles to Meridian, Mississippi, in the early 1940s.

Like most Black people in Meridian, the Summer family learned how to live with little and still enjoy life. Cloverine remembered how her father had crept into the room she shared with her sister and brother and woke them up in the early evening. In a very quiet manner, her father instructed them to get dressed. They knew because of racial tension, how to get ready to leave.

They joined their mother in the kitchen. Papa went first, opened the door and motioned everyone to lie on their belly, and start crawling out the door. They could not take the chance to stand up and walk out. No telling who was hiding in the woods.

Papa had explained that evening, that tonight would be an important night. He talked back to the White landowner about the shortage in his pay. The landowner did not like Papa asking about his money.

"He may come tonight and bring some Klu Kluxxers with him. The safest thing we can do is leave as soon as it gets dark." They all knew Papa loved them and wanted them to be safe.

They started crawling to Papa's sister's house in Meridian. They crawled some of the time on their belly, and sometimes on their hands and knees.

Papa had big dreams for Cloverine. She would attend the local Black high school and maybe even go to college. Papa knew she was naturally smart and a hard worker. He found any type of menial labor, whatever he could do to take care of his wife and three children.

One day while Cloverine was rummaging through some papers her father had, she found a paper titled "The Meridian Race Riot of (1871)." According to this article, three Black men were on trial before a White judge. Finley, also known as Tyler, shot and killed Justice Bramlette. People started shooting in the courtroom and two Black men were killed. Tyler jumped from the second floor. He was caught and shot to death by the sheriff and his posse. Large crowds of Whites and Blacks assembled in separate areas of town. Mayor Stur-

of Pennsylvania have resisted. [Applause.] Thank God, that labor, from St. Louis to Portland, has organized for resistance, for it is only the twilight and struggling dawn of a better future.

SOUTHERN OUTRAGES.

ANOTHER REBEL VERSION OF THE MERIDIAN (MISS.) MASSACRE—SEVEN PERSONS KILLED—THE MAYOR FORCED TO RESIGN AND LEAVE THE STATE.

MERIDIAN, Miss., March 7.—Yesterday, during a trial of three negroes, before Justice Bramlette, for riotous conduct, one of the prisoners, named Finley, alias Tyler, shot and instantly killed Justice Bramlette. An indiscriminate firing ensued, and two negroes were killed in the Court-room. The negro who killed the Justice jumped from a second story window, but was pursued and shot to death by the Sheriff and his posse. The citizens assembled in large numbers, and with arms, to assist the officers, and the Sheriff was commanded to disarm the negroes. In the execution of the order, several negroes were killed by the Sheriff's party during last night. The total number of persons killed, as far as positively known, is seven—six negroes and Judge Bramlette (white).

The Mayor, Wm. Sturgis, was, on his own request this morning, after tendering his resignation, given safe conduct to the cars by citizens, on his pledge to go North and never return.

STILL ANOTHER VERSION—A COLORED MEMBER OF THE LEGISLATURE MORTALLY WOUNDED.

JACKSON, March 7.—A riot occurred at Meridian, Miss., 90 miles from here, yesterday, during which Judge Bramlette of the City Court, a white man, and eight or ten negroes were killed, and a number of whites and negroes wounded. The following explanation is given of the origin of the trouble: A fire occurred on Saturday night, destroying $75,000 worth of property, and Loften, a negro, was arrested as the incendiary, and ... ... trial before Judge Bramlette, when Tyler, a ne-

(Sanders, S. (2018, January 11). *The Meridian Race Riot (1871)*. BlackPast.org. https://www.blackpast.org/african-american-history/meridian-race-riot-1871/)

*Meridian Riot of 1871 is one of the most violent days
in the history of the town.*

gis was denied support from the federal government. The sheriff was ordered to disarm the Black citizens. Six Black people were killed. Mayor Sturgis resigned and was given safe passage to an unknown northern destination. He never returned.

Reading about the Meridian Riot added fuel to the fire that was already burning in Cloverine about race relations. Cloverine already knew when she was in the 11th grade that she would not be able to work as a maid at the Holiday Inn. That was one of the best jobs in town. She cleaned rooms for a few days when she graduated. She kept her eye out, and when she heard about an opening to be the supervisor of the maids, she asked the big boss about applying.

It was not a formal application process; the Boss knew Cloverine was a hard worker, and he knew she had good relations with the other workers. He knew Cloverine was the one who organized the workers to have a way for everyone to have their childcare taken care of while they were working.

Cloverine had talked to the other maids and got them to agree to take care of all the children on their off day.

It was a simple system. There was a rotation system. On your day-off, everyone dropped their children at your home. You took care of the children, cooked breakfast and lunch, and had an afternoon snack. Usually, it was about 10 to 20 children. Just depended on who had to work what hours.

One year, Cloverine decided to stay home and take care of all the children full time. She converted her garage into a play area for the children. She called her business, Summer's Day Care and Baby-Sitting Service.

She and her helpers would drive a station wagon out into the country to pick up the children whose parents did not have a car. With the station wagon full, they would bring the children back to her home.

She told Topaz, "My sister and I had made crock-a-sac dresses to put on the children while their clothes were being washed. When we got home, we would undress the children, put on the crock-a-sac dresses, and wash the clothes they had been wearing. A lot of those children did not have running water. We would have to bathe each child. To keep the children from spreading lice and infections, I would drop a pinch of pine soil in the wash water," she told Topaz. "While their clothes were drying, we would serve breakfast, and get ready for lunch," the feisty business woman stated.

Mrs. Summer taught herself how to run the Summer Day Care and Baby-Sitting Service. "I went back to school. I took childcare and nutrition courses to get a license," she told *Meridian Newspaper*. The Summer Day Care and Baby-Sitting Service became the first licensed daycare center in Meridian.

As she grew out of space, she started to look around for a larger space. The priest at St. James Catholic Church, where she was a member, agreed to let her use the abandoned elementary school building. No rent, but she would be responsible for the building maintenance.

A lot of people criticized Cloverine for spending so much money remodeling the old school building. She told the local newspaper, "I knew God was blessing me. If I did the best I could here, he would make a better way for me."

Mrs. Summer expanded her daycare and babysitting business. She discovered a way to get an SBA (Small Business Administration) loan. It was a miracle that this information came into Mrs. Summer's hands. She had a worker, Mrs. Chimes, who took care of babies from 6-weeks-old to a year at her daycare center. Mrs. Chimes was a recognized baby lover. Her husband had a janitorial business where he cleaned business in downtown Meridian. Mr. Chimes cleaned all of the banks in Meridian. He hired his son, Chimes Jr., as one of his helpers. Junior was an alcoholic who could not hold a job anywhere else in town. Mr. Chimes hired Junior knowing that he would have to constantly check his work. This created supervisory requirements in addition to managing the five other workers he had. Mr. Chimes was a Black man running a business that required the utmost of care and concern. He was a Black man cleaning up important White people's business premises.

One night Junior was assigned the task of cleaning up a bank president's office. When Junior emptied the trash, he decided to read through what was being thrown away. He found a card from an SBA official in Columbus, Mississippi. In the drunken stupor that he always showed up at work in, he recognized the idea of SBA. "I'm saving this card for Mrs. Summer," he decided.

Junior gave the card to Mrs. Summer. She called the person listed and began the process of getting a Small Business Loan for the Summer Day Care and Baby-Sitting service.

By using a life insurance policy as collateral, she built a brand-new Summer Day Care and Baby-Sitting service on the edge of downtown Meridian in co-operation with the Mississippi branch of the SBA.

Children learning at Mrs. Summers Day Care Center.

"This had never been done before. Children stayed at home with friends and family members if their parents worked outside the home."

"I love taking care of the children. That's what God sent me here to do. I have lived a good life playing with the children," she told one reporter.

Mrs. Summer passed the business on to her children, who kept up the tradition of childcare and babysitting service.

Topaz loved Mrs. Cloverine Summer because she was an entrepreneur. She figured out a way to serve community and have income for herself. She set a great example as a community supporter and activist. From her, Topaz learned that "you got to crawl before you walk."

12

Whispers behind the Pine Trees

By Furahaa Saba

A lot of events occurred behind the Pine Trees in Meridian, Mississippi.

Mrs. Magnolia Louise Jefferson suffered a heart attack while reading an article in *Crisis Magazine.* Mrs. Jefferson had been studying and looking for her name to appear in the official N.A.A.C.P. periodical since 1940. She continued to fight the Civil Rights battle while facing fear, rejection, and personal isolation.

She died sitting in the living room of her home in her favorite wingback reading chair. The floor lamp dimly lit the floral-wall-papered front room. Her right leg was crossed over the left at the ankle.

When Able, her long-time caretaker, meandered into the room, he noticed that her small square eyeglasses were in her lap, on her dark and light green floral print dress. "Why don't you put your glasses on?," the Black man asked.

No answer.

"Ah, don't start this morning Magnolia," he complained. Abel kept mumbling, "I get tired of this. Ask you somethin' and you don't say nothin."

He heard the labored breathing, "Oh Lord please," Able begged. "Let me get the ambulance here," he prayed as he hobbled toward the 1940 mahogany telephone stand. He picked up

Crisis Magazine is the official magazine of the NAACP (National Association for the Advancement of Colored People).

the old black telephone receiver and dialed operator, "Hello Central" he pleaded, "Get me an ambulance for Mrs. Magnolia Jefferson. Hurry." There was no need to give an address or directions. Everyone in Meridian knew where Mrs. Magnolia Louise Jefferson lived, "That place over there behind the tall pine trees."

Mrs. Magnolia Jefferson took her last deep breath with a subtle smile and died.

"I told you not to do this," Able cried. "I don't want to be in here with you by myself and you ain't here." Able fell on his good right knee and called the deepest voice of God within himself that he could reach. The truth sank in.

By the time the ambulance and onlookers arrived at the pine-shaded home, Able had composed himself. He met them at the faded white gate. He crept down the pine scented gray concrete walkway, kicking pinecones with his walking stick.

"Call the coroner," he told the senior-most-looking White person in charge.

"What happened? Did she seem unusual? Was she sick? Is there any other family? Are you family? Did he just finally get tired and kill that old woman?" Were some of the questions floating in the air.

Able did not answer any of the questions. Instead, he cast his dark brown eyes down toward Mother Earth, then back up to the crowd. These are official and unofficial, nosy, and genuinely concerned people, he surmised. He projected the deep sadness, respect, dignity, and love he thought the situation required.

Able let the medics supervisor into the house before he went to his sparse cabin in the back of the main house. There was no one to call except friends. All in her family—her husband, two sons, and one daughter, and her parents—everybody in her family was gone to glory. "I hope you with your family tonight," Able prayed.

Able sat through the funeral and NAACP (National Association for the Advancement of Colored People) committee meeting like a corpse. Everyone kept saying the same thing. "At least she died at home. She ain't been out of that house in twenty-five years."

Mrs. Magnolia Louis Jefferson died of heart ailment partly because she refused to leave her home to go to a doctor. Her only contact with people outside of Able was with the few friends who were brave enough to venture behind the pine trees. A guest entering the Jefferson home had to be ready to encounter the extensive intellectual environment Mrs. Jefferson actively sought. The books, magazines, and pamphlets that lined the walls, floors, chairs, and every possible empty space, related to Mrs. Jefferson's interest: flowers, herbal practices, and civil rights.

If you were a registered Democratic Black Meridian voter, you could expect to hear from Mrs. Jefferson by telephone during any election. She was known to call on any politician regardless of party, from Meridian to the White House, to explain her take on issues that she thought they were overlooking. "You know Mister, we need more money in the Black School District." "We need you to support the Civil Rights Legislation," she wired, called, and harassed anyone remotely involved. She was an avid reader and would call any person of political influence, elected or non-elected, to make sure they thoroughly understood her point of view as an economically poor Black woman from Meridian, Mississippi.

"This is Mrs. Magnolia Louise Jefferson," she would begin whether in her neighborhood, city hall, state capitol, or the White House. "I'm calling because I don't leave my house. Ever since the Ku Klux Klan called my floral shop and told me they would blow me up if they ever caught me in the street again. I closed my business that day. I had all my flowers moved to my house. They call here and threaten all the time. 'If you come outside those pine trees, we gonna kill you,' is what they say. So that's the reason I'm calling you rather than coming to see you. I want you to know that Proposition "xxx" is against the constitutional rights of the people in Mississippi. I want you to vote no. Even though I don't leave the house, I can get a protest in front of your office for you to understand better."

For Black people, in and out of her neighborhood, she had a different message, "I have some Literature for you honey, the *Crisis Magazine*. It's from the NAACP (you know the National Association for the Advancement of Colored People) magazine and from the Meridian Negro News. It will help you understand what is at stake. We need you to come out and vote. Help keep the Democrats in office, we stand a better chance. So much needs to be done. You know you the only one that can teach your children. We can't trust these white people to educate us. I'll have Amos bring it over to you. You know I don't leave the house, ever since the KKK threatened to blow me up if they ever caught me in the street…," she would repeat before thanking the party for listening.

The heart attack Mrs. Jefferson suffered resulted from years of worrying and praying about the condition of herself and Black people.

The Civil Rights Movement was her family. "They treat me like a stepchild," she would complain behind the pine trees. She felt like an outsider in the NAACP circles. When she sent her voice out in public by telephone she would shout their accolades, "If it wasn't for the Civil Rights Movement, we would still be back in the1800s," she declared to people on her daily calls about civil rights issues.

Able pondered all these thoughts as he decided how to dispose of Mrs. Jefferson's estate. "She don't have no children. All her children are in these books, and papers. She don't have no man but me, and God know she wasn't my woman. I never even touched her in a private way. Well Lord," he signed, shifting in the old squeaky rocking chair, "It's in your hands. I just don't know what to do."

The telephone rang often interrupting Able's thoughts.

"Yes, I'm fine." He assured all callers, including his daughter that he had by his only girlfriend.

"No baby, ain't no use in your coming down here. Miss Magnolia is gone, and I'm here all alone, except for God. You stay there and take care of your Mama. How she doin' any way?"

"Papa, she doin' fine, except for what the doctors say," his daughter Ann would begin the litany. "You know she had that stroke, she got high blood pressure and diabetes. But she won't stop eating junk and smoking them nasty cigarettes. I'm doing the best I can, Daddy, but she doesn't care," the abandoned daughter confessed.

That sealed the deal for Able. He thought, "I don't care either that's my problem. I just don't care about nobody on this earth. Mama and Papa gone. All my sisters and brothers are gone. Why am I here?"—the old man pondered.

The smell of pine trees woke Able one more morning. It was a day when he would have gone shopping for Mrs. Jefferson. "But she ain't here," he remembered.

If Mrs. Jefferson had been alive, she would have instructed Able, "Bring in my valerian root tea, my heart feels heavy today. While you're doing that, you may as well bring in the burdock root. That's my favorite. Don't forget to get the maple syrup from the health food store."

Able thought about how he would grunt and complain. "You ought to go to a doctor."

"They don't know no more about me than I do," Mrs. Jefferson would argue. "Truth is, you have to take care of your own health," the frail women disputed.

Knowing he could not win the argument, Able would change the subject. "Well, you ought to at least come and let me take you for a drive," he challenged the reclusive woman.

Tension would rise to the ceiling in the room before Mrs. Jefferson spoke. Balling up her fists and tightening every available facial muscle, Mrs. Jefferson would declare, "You know them Ku Kluxers threatened to blow me up if they ever caught me in public. They are willing to take my life, just because I can show people how to vote. We have a right to vote. We fought for and won our freedom long ago. Did you see what they did to those children in that Birmingham Church? Such cowards, bombing children in a church. Able, I know you remember what happened right here in Meridian. Look how they killed those three civil rights workers. They were just beginning to get things going. Ain't no need for me to leave this house. They will have to come through those pine trees, and burn everything before they get to me," she constantly repeated.

Able took a deep breath each time he remembered the daily conversation. He had not been able to help Mrs. Jefferson release her fear. She persisted in living her whole life around this very real threat.

All Able could do was run her errands and negotiate all external affairs that required face-to-face communication. In private he prayed for Mrs. Jefferson's liberation. It never came that he could see.

After months of reading, praying, cleaning, writing, Able discovered his own plan for freedom. He woke up before daylight the following Monday morning. He had given himself the weekend to think things over. He was waiting in his tan 1960 Chevrolet for the bank to open. Able went inside and liquidated every asset he could from his own accounts and those of Mrs. Magnolia Louise Jefferson. He went to two other banks and conducted the same business. His last stop was a bank where the safety deposit box was located.

Able had not bothered to go there before, because he knew Mrs. Jefferson's last will and testament was stored there. He did not bother to read it. He simply took the papers and jewels that were generously displayed in the large gray metal storage box and put them in his pockets. He had to use every pocket he had because Mrs. Jefferson loved jewels. Able left the private viewing area, and returned the box to the clerk. He did not bother to close the account. He did not want to alarm anyone.

Slowly, Able drove the few miles back through Meridian to the Jefferson estate. He drove the same route he had been using for over 50 years, straight through the heart of downtown Meridian. He looked everything over carefully. He looked at the tallest building in town, known as "The Three-Foot Building"; it was an office complex. He saw the old Marks Rothenberg building, a historical landmark. He noticed the Opera House that had been under renovation for at least 25 years. He recalled the hysteria that occurred at the old Kress store, because some colored people wanted to sit at the counter and have lunch. He looked to his right and saw the statue of the confederate soldier, a name he did not know. Oh, there were so many memories. There was the police station and city hall. Able looked at all of them, and regretted the fact that this was the only town he knew.

As was his habit, Amos drove about 10 miles an hour through town on the busiest street in Meridian. He always hogged two lanes. Several pine trees lined the road and Able rolled down his window to smell the pleasant faint aroma of pine in the air.

When he arrived at the Jefferson home, he parked the car in the front. "Maybe somebody can use it," he thought. This was the first visible sign of a different day in the Jefferson home behind the pine trees. The car was never parked in front of the house.

Able got out of the car as slowly as he drove. Carefully he took his cane and went in the front door. "I ought to go out to the cottage to see how it is," he thought. "No," he decided. "It's alright."

He simply went into the front parlor and sat down in his old chair. Able looked over at the chair that Mrs. Jefferson always occupied. With deliberate pace, he moved over to the chair and pulled up the *Crisis Magazine* that she was reading when she had the heart attack. Able rolled the magazine up as if it were a newspaper. He walked to the mantle over the fireplace that had not worked in 30 years. He walked through the whole house one last time. "I'm leavin'," he declared.

Able turned and walked away the same way he came in the last time. He inhaled the smell of the pine trees one more time as he walked through the densely wooded area.

The community began whispering. "Ain't nobody seen Able.".

Able walked faster than he drove. He literally walked off into the sunset.

The community continued to whisper behind the pine trees. It did not matter. What did matter was the fact that a committee of Black and White citizens from the Meridian Historical Society recognized the importance of the information Mrs. Jefferson had collected. They came together and created the Magnolia Louise Jefferson Memorial Home. It stands as a historical marker of the place that was used to advance voter registration in Meridian.

The years of hard work by the committee was one more step toward racial understanding and respect, and voter registration.

Even though there was a lot of whispering behind the pine trees. It did not matter. The truth rests in each person's perspective.